L.E.A.D.S.S.

EQUIPPING LEADERS
FOR GENERATIONAL IMPACT

DARRELL JACKSON

AND BRYANT LEE SR.

L.E.A.D.S.S.

Equipping Leaders for Generational Impact

PARTICIPANT MANUAL

Author / Workbook Design: Darrell Jackson
Co-Author: Bryant Lee Sr.
Editor: Joseph Chinn
Contributors: Terrance R. Samuels and Kenneth Basile
Cover Design: Anointing Productions
Interior Layout & Development: Raise Performance Group

Ergon Publishing
PO Box 709
Fresno, Texas 77545
www.raiseperformancegroup.com

ISBN: 979-8-218-85069-2

1st Edition / 2025

Table of Contents

Table of Contents Continued

Welcome to the RPG Leadership Development Course

Welcome to L.E.A.D.S.S. (Lead, Equip, Align, Design, Serve, Secure), a comprehensive leadership development course by Raise Performance Group designed to cultivate healthy leaders, strengthen church systems, and expand Kingdom impact. This course unites spiritual formation and strategic leadership, providing a clear framework for developing sustainable ministries and healthy teams.

Built upon the six pillars of the RPG Leadership Framework, each session focuses on a key dimension of effective ministry leadership:

1. **Lead with Clarity** – Seeing Clearly. Speaking Confidently. Serving Daily.
2. **Equip Disciples** – Empowering Others for Greater Impact.
3. **Align Systems** – Building Healthy Systems for Sustainable Growth.
4. **Design for Growth** – Creating Pathways for Spiritual Maturity.
5. **Serve the World** – Developing a Missional Mindset.
6. **Secure the Future** – Building for Long-Term Kingdom Impact.

Each session combines biblical teaching, practical workshops, and strategic planning exercises designed to help participants apply learning within their local ministry context. Participants are encouraged to engage actively, complete all assigned reflections and templates, and collaborate with peers for maximum impact. This shared learning process creates an environment of growth, accountability, and encouragement as leaders refine their vision and strategy.

Our team believes that the truest expression of leadership is faithful stewardship and humble service, developing what God has entrusted to your care and generously investing it in the lives of others. As you embark on this journey, we pray that your time in this training will inspire and equip you to lead with clarity, serve with humility, and build ministries that remain steadfast and fruitful for the glory of God.

In His Service and for His Glory,
The Lead Team at Raise Performance Group

Overview

The L.E.A.D.S.S. Framework

L.E.A.D.S.S. is a six-pillar, biblically grounded framework designed to equip leaders to build healthy ministries, develop mature disciples, and create Kingdom impact that lasts from generation to generation.

1. **Lead With Clarity: See Clearly. Speak Confidently. Serve Daily. -** Know where God is leading and communicate it with conviction so others can follow with confidence.
2. **Equip Disciples: Empowering Others For Greater Impact -** Develop and empower people to grow spiritually and lead others, multiplying ministry impact.
3. **Align Systems: Healthy Systems That Build Healthy Ministries -** Build simple, healthy structures and processes that support ministry growth and prevent burnout.
4. **Design for Growth: Creating Pathways for Spiritual Maturity -** Create intentional pathways that guide believers from new faith to spiritual maturity and leadership.
5. **Serve the World: Developing a Missional Mindset -** Mobilize disciples to live on mission daily, serving others, and sharing the Gospel locally and globally.
6. **Secure the Future: Built Biblically For Kingdom Impact -** Integrate people, systems, and vision into a unified strategy that lasts beyond you and strengthens future generations.

Our Purpose

The primary goal is to help align your leadership with God's vision for your ministry. By the end of our time together, you will be equipped to:

- Build systems to increase ministry effectiveness and simplicity.
- Create pathways for spiritual growth and maturity within your congregation.
- Develop people who multiply disciples and leaders.
- Engage your community with the hope of the Gospel.

Who This Manual Is For

This training is designed for:

- **Pastors & Key Leaders:** Lead pastors, ministers, deacons, executive leaders, and other decision-makers shaping the church's vision and strategy.

- **Lay Leaders:** Small group leaders, ministry servants, and emerging leaders who serve on the frontlines of ministry.

How to Use This Manual

This manual functions as both a personal guide and a record of your corporate growth. You have the flexibility to set your own pace, but each session is designed to last approximately 150 minutes.

Each session includes:

1. **Workshops** to apply principles directly to your ministry.
2. **Action Plans** to guide your next steps.
3. **Reflection Sections** to help you process and adjust along the way.
4. **L.E.A.D.S.S. In Action** sections help you put each session into practice through real ministry activities. These sections are divided into two parts:

   - **Personal Engagement (Required Activities):** These are the core assignments every participant must complete to apply the session content. They help you practice each principle, build habits, and move your ministry forward between sessions.

   - **Group Engagement (Optional Activities if Available):** If offered in your cohort, these activities provide added support through peer interaction, coaching calls, or discussion portals. They are optional and may vary by group, but are designed to deepen learning and encourage collaborative feedback.

IMPORTANT NOTE: There are templates that accompany sessions 1 - 6. Scan the QR Code that is located in the "Contact Us" section on page 111 of this training manual to gain access to the RPG Templates.

Overview Continued

My Notes Section

A **My Notes** section has been created at the end of Sessions 1-6 as a space to reflect on the workshops, action plans, reflection and L.E.A.D.S.S. in Action sections of each preceding session.

You may include any additional questions that you would like to remember ahead of the upcoming session, or use this area to jot down key ideas that you intend to discuss or implement with your lead team, church staff or church members.

Our Unique Learn, Link, Lead Method

Every lesson in each session is built around the **Learn**, **Link**, and **Lead** method. This method moves leaders from biblical truth to action and measurable impact. It ensures that you:

- **Learn** biblical foundations and principles.
- **Link** the teaching to your unique ministry context.
- **Lead** through practical and measurable action steps.

At the conclusion of Session Six, participants will present a Church Strengthening Plan that synthesizes all six leadership pillars. This plan is designed to be Spirit-led and actionable, enabling immediate implementation in each participant's context.

Session 1

LEAD WITH CLARITY

SEE CLEARLY. SPEAK CONFIDENTLY. SERVE DAILY.

PROVERBS 29:18

Objective:

To equip leaders with relevant tools to help them discern and articulate a clear, God-centered vision for their ministry. Participants will learn to define vision, mission, and values aligned with biblical principles, and create a Ministry Vision Map that provides direction, unity, and daily focus for their teams.

 ## 1.0 – Introduction

Every enduring ministry begins with clarity about vision, mission, and values (VMV)—three essentials that guide a church's identity, direction, and culture. Vision reveals where God is leading. Mission defines what God calls us to do. Values express how we behave while accomplishing the mission. When leaders anchor these key elements in Scripture, the church moves with unity, purpose, and spiritual authority.

- **Vision** is a clear, compelling picture of the future God is calling your ministry to pursue. It describes where you are going and what the ministry will become when God's purposes are fulfilled. It answers the question, "Where is God leading us?" A strong vision brings focus, passion, and alignment to every part of the church.[1]

- **Mission** defines why the ministry exists. It identifies the core assignment God has given the church—what you must faithfully do every day in order to fulfill His purpose. Mission is active, directional, and measurable, keeping the church centered on its biblical calling.[2] It answers the question, "What has God called us to faithfully do," and it flows from the Great Commission (Matthew 28:18-20).

- **Values** define the attitudes, commitments, and behaviors that guide how a church lives out its mission. They answer, "How will we conduct ourselves as we follow Jesus together?" Values shape culture, influence decisions, set expectations for leaders, and reveal the true identity of the church. They are not wishful ideals—they are the convictions that show who the church really is.[3]

Emphasizing the importance of spiritual character in leadership, J. Oswald Sanders notes that true leadership effectiveness flows from a leader's inner life, not merely outward skill.[4] His insight reminds us that leadership is formed in private devotion before it is displayed in public responsibility—and that this inner life is essential for vision, mission, and values to take root and endure.

01

Jesus modeled this pattern throughout His ministry. He prayed before launching His public work, before selecting His disciples, and before making critical decisions (Luke 6:12; Mark 1:35). His example shows that biblical leadership begins in the secret place—not on the stage. When leaders see clearly, they lead clearly.

Dr. Tony Evans further notes that Kingdom vision aligns earthly leadership under heaven's authority, shaping leaders who build God's Church instead of personal platforms.[5] Throughout Scripture, God consistently provided direction before commissioning His leaders:

- Moses received a vision of deliverance before leaving Egypt (Exodus 3:7-10).
- Nehemiah saw the broken walls before he began rebuilding (Nehemiah 2:11-18).
- Daniel and his Hebrew friends remained integral in the midst of a tempting culture (Daniel 1).
- Paul understood his mission to the Gentiles before taking his first journey (Acts 9:15-16).

When vision, mission, and values are rooted in Scripture and led by the Spirit, they form the foundation that guides leaders and unifies God's people toward generational impact. Without them, ministries drift, leaders burn out, and discipleship weakens.

In the session, you will learn to discern God's direction for your ministry, turn it into a clear vision and mission, and communicate it in a way that inspires action.

Biblical Story Highlight – Nehemiah's Vision Clarity

Let's take a moment to review Nehemiah's leadership. Read Nehemiah 1:1-2:18, and next to the bullet points below, list the key actions Nehemiah took before casting the vision to his leaders. We will discuss your answers together once you have completed the exercise.

-
-
-
-
-

After hearing the devastating news about his hometown, Nehemiah felt the burden, prayed, assessed the situation, and then cast a vision for the people to carry out. Remember, having a Burden + Prayer + Assessment + Vision + Action is a great model for leading with clarity.

1.1 – LEARN: Discover God's Blueprint for Your Ministry

Introduction to LEARN

Today, we focus on learning essential truths and leadership principles from God's Word. This section reminds us of what Scripture teaches about leadership and encourages us to ground our leadership in biblical truth rather than in shifting trends.

NOTE: *These sessions will realign hearts, clarify goals, and invite the Holy Spirit's guidance back into the center of ministry work.*

Key Scriptures & Insights with Practical Tips
Let's begin by taking time to review some key scriptures and foundational insights that will assist you in leading with clarity.

1. **Vision as Spiritual Necessity – Proverbs 29:18**
   When there is no clear direction, people lose focus, discipline, and purpose. Leaders who operate without a fresh or clear vision often find their teams confused or unmotivated. In Proverbs 29:18, we discover that God's clear revelation provides a sense of joy and direction, and keeps us from drifting into self-led agendas.

   - **Cross References:** 1 Samuel 3:1; Amos 8:11-12; Ephesians 1:15-23; Psalm 1:1-2; 119:2; John 13:17

   - **Practical Tip:** Schedule quarterly "vision checks" with your team. Ask them:

     ▷ Are our current activities aligned with God's direction?

     ▷ Have we drifted into busyness instead of obedience?

     ▷ What adjustments do we need to make to refocus on our God-given purpose?

2. **Write the Vision – Habakkuk 2:2-3**

   God calls leaders to make vision clear and visible so others can follow it. Writing the vision turns divine direction into shared purpose and helps keep everyone moving in unity. In Habakkuk 2:2-3, God commanded Habakkuk to make the vision plain by writing it, so that others who read it could understand and share it.

   - **Cross References:** Deuteronomy 6:6-9; Psalm 119:105; Revelation 1:19; 21:5

   - **Practical Tip:** Display and share your vision where leaders frequently gather (e.g., meeting rooms, bulletin boards, volunteer handbooks, in worship services, etc.), so that it becomes an integral part of daily ministry life.

3. **Vision that Mobilizes – Nehemiah 2:17-20**

   A God-given vision moves people from watching to working. When vision connects to real needs and God's faithfulness, it stirs hearts to action and unites the church in purpose. In Nehemiah 2:17-20, Nehemiah linked the vision to people's needs and God's faithfulness.

   - **Cross References:** Exodus 35:20-29; 36:1-7; Matthew 4:18-22

   - **Practical Tip:** When casting vision, always connect it to a story, testimony, or clear cause, because people follow visions that resonate with their hearts.

4. **God's Vision Is Bigger Than You – Ephesians 3:20-21**

   God's plans will always stretch us beyond what we can do alone. Vision should stretch your faith and require God's power, not just your ability. God's vision calls us to depend on His power, trust His timing, and believe He can do more through us than we could ever imagine. In Ephesians 3:20-21, Paul reminds us to trust and celebrate the God Who alone is able to fulfill the vision He gives.

   - **Cross References:** Joshua 1:1-9; 6:1-11; Hebrews 11:30

   - **Practical Tip:** Include at least one significant goal in your vision, something that can only be achieved with God's help and guidance.

 **LET'S REFLECT ... LET'S TALK**

Individual Reflection Questions – LEARN

1. What has God revealed to me about my ministry's future through Scripture or prayer recently?

2. Which part of my current vision is most aligned with God's heart? Which part may need refining?

3. How often am I personally seeking God for direction instead of just making plans?

Team Discussion Questions – LEARN

1. Do we as a team share the same biblical understanding of our mission?

2. How do we know our vision comes from God and not just human ambition?

3. What biblical leaders inspire us in casting a clear vision? Why?

 ## 1.2 – LINK: Connecting Truth to Your Context

Introduction to LINK

Vision should shape your culture, systems, preaching, leadership, and decision-making; not just sit in a binder. In this section, we will anchor biblical truths to your ministry setting. At your tables, you will address your church's current reality using guided questions and small-group collaboration.

Classroom Contextualization Process

This activity helps leaders connect the church's stated vision and mission to its current reality and ministry practices. Each step is designed to move from reflection to realignment so that your vision and mission are not just written statements, but living guides that shape the direction of your ministry.

 ### Step 1 – Assess Your Current Reality (10 min)

Objective: This exercise helps you identify how clearly your vision and mission are understood and practiced.

- Write your current vision and mission statements on a whiteboard or large sheet of paper where everyone can see them.

Discuss Briefly:

- When was the last time your team taught or intentionally communicated this to your congregation? Explain.

- Can everyone recite the vision or mission from memory?

- Does this mission feel alive and central, or is it something people rarely reference?

01

Step 2 – Identify Gaps (10 min)

Objective: This exercise helps you evaluate alignment between what you say and what you actually do.

- Compare your stated mission with your current ministry practices. Circle areas where alignment is strong and underline areas where it is weak or unclear.

Discuss Briefly:

- If discipleship is a core priority, where is it visibly happening? Explain.

- Which ministries or activities do not reflect your stated mission?

Step 3 – Engage Others in Discernment (15 min)

Objective: This exercise helps you discern where God is moving in your ministry and where human tendencies may be shaping your direction. Involve multiple perspectives to recognize where God is already at work.

- Break into pairs/small groups and share your vision and mission statements aloud.

Discuss Briefly:

- For 2 minutes, each partner will ask the other person two guiding questions:

  ▷ Where do you see God's fingerprints, evidence of His leading and blessing?

  ▷ Where do you see human fingerprints, areas driven more by habit, pressure, or preference?

- After 4-5 minutes, we will come back together and collect highlights from each discussion. Identify 1-2 "God fingerprints" worth celebrating, and 1-2 "Human fingerprints" needing prayer and adjustment.

 Step 4 – Discern Cultural & Community Needs (15 min)

Objective: Connect your vision and mission to the real needs of the people you serve.

- List the top three needs in your surrounding community, one spiritual, one emotional, and one practical (e.g., family support, youth engagement, poverty, grief care, etc.).

Discuss Briefly:

- How does our vision or mission currently speak to these needs?

- What adjustments or ministries might help us connect better with these realities?

Read: Acts 17:22-23 – Notice how Paul began by connecting with the people's existing beliefs and culture before introducing the Gospel.

Reflect – How can we follow Paul's example in contextualizing our ministry to reach people where they are?

 **LET'S REFLECT ... LET'S TALK**

Individual Reflection Questions – LINK

1. What is one area where our stated mission and actual ministry practice don't align?

2. How well do I understand my community's current needs and culture?

3. Who else should be at the table as we refine our vision?

Team Discussion Questions – LINK

1. Are we clear about the difference between our vision and our mission?

2. Where have we allowed traditions or old programs to drift from our vision?

3. How can we better listen to both God and our community when clarifying direction?

 1.3 – LEAD: Putting Vision Into Action

Introduction to LEAD

Now, we will move from inspiration to execution, because "clarity without action" is just theory. Take the insights you have learned in the LINK section about your ministry and create a Vision Map to implement immediately.

Action Steps & Workshop Activity – Vision Map Creation (40 min)

- **Step 1 – Seek God's Direction in Prayer (5 min)**

  Quiet reflection: Ask God to reveal one adjustment to your current vision.

- **Step 2 – Draft/Refine Vision & Mission Statements (10 min)**

  Write your vision in one sentence, and your mission in one sentence.

- **Step 3 – Define 3-5 Core Values (10 min)**

  Choose values that shape your church's culture. Add Scripture references for each.

- **Step 4 – Create a Vision Communication Plan (10 min)**

  List at least 3-4 ways you will articulate, exemplify, and reinforce the vision in sermons, meetings, and everyday conversations.

- **Step 5 – Share & Get Feedback (5 min)**

  Pair up with someone at your table, and present your Vision Map in 2-3 minutes to receive input.

 **LET'S REFLECT ... LET'S TALK**

Individual Reflection Questions – LEAD

1. What's the first step I can take this week to move our vision forward?

2. How will I keep vision casting from becoming just a "once-a-year" sermon/focus?

3. What's one value I must personally model for the vision to be credible?

Team Discussion Questions – LEAD

1. How can we incorporate vision communication into our worship services and regular meetings?

2. What practical changes will show our congregation that we are serious about our vision?

3. How will we measure progress toward fulfilling our vision?

> **Suggested Resources**
>
> - 30-Day Vision Communication Plan (RPG Resource)
> - Vision Clarity Conversation Template (RPG Resource)
> - Vision Framing Template (RPG Resource)
> - Visioneering by Andy Stanley
>
> **NOTE:** Scan the QR code on page 111 to download the RPG templates.

 ## 1.4 – L.E.A.D.S.S. In Action

Personal Engagement (Required Activities)

1. Write your Vision and Mission statements (no more than two sentences each) and spend time reflecting on Matthew 28:18-20.
2. List your Core Values with 1-2 supporting Bible verses.
3. Use the 30-Day Vision Communication Template to create a plan with at least three communication touch-points.
4. Have a "Vision Clarity Conversation" with at least three team members and record their feedback.

Group Engagement (Optional Activities if Available)

1. Share your Vision and Mission statements in the group portal for feedback.
2. Join a 30-minute group coaching call and note three key takeaways.

End Notes

Session 1 - Endnotes (Lead With Clarity)

1. Henry Blackaby & Richard Blackaby, *Spiritual Leadership: Moving People on to God's Agenda* (B&H Publishing, 2011).

2. Aubrey Malphurs, *Developing a Vision for Ministry in the 21st Century* (Baker Books, 2015).

3. Patrick Lencioni, *The Advantage: Why Organizational Health Trumps Everything Else in Business* (San Francisco: Jossey-Bass, 2012).

4. J. Oswald Sanders, Spiritual Leadership: Principles of Excellence for Every Believer (Chicago: Moody Publishers, 2007).

5. Tony Evans, *The Kingdom Agenda: Life Under God* (Chicago: Moody Publishers, 2006).

6. Key Scripture references used in Session 1 include: Proverbs 29:18; Habakkuk 2:2-3; Luke 6:12; Mark 1:35; Exodus 3:7-10; Nehemiah 2:11-18; Acts 9:15-16; 1 Samuel 3:1; Amos 8:11-12; Ephesians 1:15-23; Psalm 1:1-2; Psalm 119:2; John 13:17.

7. General framework on mission, vision, and values in this session were influenced by:

   - Aubrey Malphurs, *Developing a Vision for Ministry in the 21st Century* (Grand Rapids, MI: Baker Books, 1999).
   - Henry & Richard Blackaby, *Spiritual Leadership* (Nashville, TN: B&H Publishing, 2011).
   - Patrick Lencioni, *The Advantage* (San Francisco, CA: Jossey-Bass, 2012).

My Notes

Session 2

EQUIP DISCIPLES

EMPOWERING OTHERS FOR GREATER IMPACT
EPHESIANS 4:11–16

Objective:

To develop leaders who can multiply others through intentional discipleship and structured leadership development. Participants will identify the stages of a leadership pipeline and design a personalized Leader Development Pathway that empowers others for ministry effectiveness and long-term growth.

🔍 Session 1 Review - Lead With Clarity

Before we move forward, let's revisit the foundational commission to make disciples, and the importance of aligning our vision, mission, and values with God's call. This ensures every leader is moving in the same direction, and every ministry effort is aimed at fulfilling the Great Commission.

Group Debrief (15-20 min)

1. **L.E.A.D.S.S. In Action Check-In and Peer Feedback (10 minutes)**

   - Share any insights from your meditation time.
   - Briefly share the feedback you received from the Vision Clarity Conversations.
   - Share at least two ways you have seen God move since Session One began.

2. **Peer Feedback (10 minutes)**

   - Briefly explain your 30-Day Vision Communication Plan in 2 minutes.

Session 1 Summary

Session One helped us clarify the call "to make disciples" that Jesus has given to every believer. We aligned our vision with His mission, identified specific individuals in our lives to invest in, and created a practical plan to get started.

In Session Two, we will learn how to offer support to leaders and teams; thereby strengthening and multiplying disciple-making.

 ## 2.0 – Introduction

Jesus' final command to His followers was to "make disciples" (Matthew 28:18-20), establishing disciple-making as the Church's central mission. A disciple is someone who:

- Follows Jesus (Matthew 4:19),
- Learns His ways (Matthew 11:29),
- Obeys Him and Reflects His character (John 14:15; Luke 6:40), and
- Helps others do the same (Matthew 28:19-20).

Equipping disciples is more than sharing information—it means training believers to obey and live out Jesus' teachings in everyday life (2 Timothy 2:2). Jesus modeled this by focusing not on the crowds, but on intentionally developing a few who would multiply His mission.[1]

Paul emphasizes this responsibility in Ephesians 4:11-16, reminding us that leaders are not called to do all the ministry themselves, but to equip others to grow, serve, and multiply. Healthy churches are those filled with equipped disciples who live out this mission.

Biblical Story Highlight – The Church's Responsibility

Let's revisit Paul's teaching to the Ephesians. Read Ephesians 4:11-16, and next to the bullet points provided, identify the key responsibilities Paul gives to both church leaders and members. Consider how each role contributes to the church's growth and unity. After completing your notes, we will review and discuss your findings together.

-
-
-
-
-

In Ephesians 4:11-16, Paul teaches that every believer has a role in Christ's Body. Leaders equip others for ministry, and members grow, serve, and build up the church in love. When each part does its work, the church becomes strong, unified, and effective in fulfilling God's mission.

 ## 2.1 – LEARN: The Biblical Mandate for Equipping

Introduction to LEARN

Great leaders don't just lead, they multiply. This section reminds us that effective leadership begins with biblical truth, and not human trends. When we follow God's pattern, leaders grow and multiply biblically, and God's Kingdom impact grows exponentially.

Key Scriptures & Insights with Practical Tips

Let's begin by taking time to review some key scriptures and foundational insights that will assist you in equipping and empowering disciples.

1. **Equipping is a Leadership Mandate – Matthew 28:20a**

   God calls every leader to prepare and empower others for ministry. Equipping is a core responsibility of every spiritual leader. In Matthew 28:20a, Jesus commands His followers to teach others to obey all He has commanded, showing that true leadership is not just about leading people but developing them to lead and live faithfully.

   - **Cross References:** 2 Timothy 2:2; Colossians 1:28-29

   - **Practical Tip:** Create a list of all the ministry tasks you are currently doing and identify which ones you could train someone else to do within the next 60 days.

2. **Multiplication Over Addition – 2 Timothy 2:2**

   Healthy leadership focuses on developing leaders who develop others. Instead of just adding followers, multiplication happens when trained leaders reproduce more leaders, creating exponential growth for the Kingdom. In 2 Timothy 2:2, Paul instructed Timothy to entrust the Gospel to faithful people who would faithfully teach others.

   - **Cross References:** Mark 3:14-19; Acts 14:21-28; Matthew 28:18-20; Deuteronomy 4:9

   - **Practical Tip:** Always train with the expectation that the person you are training will also train someone else.

3. **Delegation Frees Leaders to Focus on Calling – Acts 6:1-7**

   Delegation allows leaders to share responsibility with others so they can focus on what God has specifically called them to do. By trusting capable people to handle tasks, leaders create space to pray, plan, and lead with greater clarity and purpose. In Acts 6:1-7, the apostles released others to serve so they could focus on prayer and the ministry of the Word.

   - **Cross References:** Exodus 18:13-26; Deuteronomy 1:13-15; Titus 1:5

   - **Practical Tip:** Start small by delegating a clearly defined, low-risk responsibility to someone and coaching them through it.

4. **Spiritual Maturity Produces Service – Hebrews 5:12-14**

   As believers grow in their faith, they naturally begin to serve others. True maturity is not measured by knowledge alone, but by a willingness to meet needs, love people, and use one's gifts to build up the Body of Christ. In Hebrews 5:12-14, spiritual maturity is marked by moving from being served to serving others.

   - **Cross References:** Matthew 20:26-28; Mark 10:44-45; John 13:1-5, 12-17, 34-35

   - **Practical Tip:** Utilize serving roles as discipleship tools by pairing people with mentors who model godly character while serving together in ministry.

 **LET'S REFLECT … LET'S TALK**

Individual Reflection Questions – LEARN

1. Am I equipping others, or am I simply doing ministry myself? Who am I currently discipling?

2. Who is one person I could begin to mentor this month?

3. What barriers keep me from delegating ministry to others?

Team Discussion Questions – LEARN

1. Are we currently multiplying leaders or just filling positions?

2. How can we create an expectation that everyone is called to serve?

3. What would change in our ministry if every leader were also mentoring someone?

2.2 – LINK: Connecting the Call to Equip with Our Context

Introduction to LINK

In this section, we shift from biblical principles to practical action, focusing on what equipping looks like in the everyday life and context of our church.

Classroom Contextualization Process

Use this section to look at your ministry with honest eyes, so to speak. Here, we evaluate how equipping is actually happening in your ministry environment. Rather than only knowing the "why," this step strengthens the "how" by identifying strengths, gaps, and opportunities to develop people, not just deliver content.

Step 1 – Assess Your Current Reality (10 min)

Objective: Identify all active ministry roles and highlight areas lacking support or succession.

- On a worksheet, list every ministry role in your church, from greeting to worship team to teaching.
- Circle which roles currently have no backup or apprentice.

Discuss Briefly:

- Which ministry roles are currently the most vulnerable if a leader steps down?

- What roles do we tend to overlook or underestimate in importance?

Step 2 – Identify Current Equipping Practices (10 min)

Objective: Evaluate how people are currently trained and pinpoint strengths and weaknesses in your equipping methods.

- How do people learn their role now: formal training, shadowing, or "sink or swim"?

Discuss Briefly:

- How effective is our current approach in preparing people for ministry? What's working? What's missing?

- What equipping methods could we add or improve to strengthen our leaders?

Step 3 – Spot the Leadership Pipeline Gaps (15 min)

Objective: Visualize your church's leadership development flow and identify where people stagnate in growth or advancement.

- Draw a simple diagram illustrating how people typically progress from being a visitor, to servant, then to leader.

Discuss Briefly:

- Where do most people in our church get "stuck" in the discipleship or leadership journey?

- What barriers or missing steps could we remove to help people grow into leadership?

02

 Step 4 – Match Leaders to Potential Apprentices (10 min)

Objective: Select potential emerging leaders and outline the specific skills or experiences they need for future leadership roles.

- Choose 1-2 people in your ministry who could take on more responsibility.
- List specific skills or experiences they need before they can lead.

Discuss Briefly:

- Who shows potential but hasn't yet been invited to lead?

- What intentional steps can we take this month to help them grow into leadership?

LET'S REFLECT ... LET'S TALK

Individual Reflection Questions – LINK

1. Where is my ministry pipeline broken or missing steps?

2. Do I have apprentices in place for my current leaders?

3. How intentional is our church about developing people, not just filling positions?

Team Discussion Questions – LINK

1. What are the top 3 ministries that need immediate leader development?

2. How can we incorporate leader-equipping into our church culture?

3. Who in our church shows potential for greater leadership?

 2.3 – LEAD: Building a Discipleship Pathway that Equips Leaders

Introduction to LEAD

In this section, we turn what we have learned and linked to our ministry into a tangible, actionable discipleship and leadership development plan. This is where we build a system that equips and moves people from a first-time guest to disciple-makers.

Workshop Activity – Discipleship Pathway Planning (40-45 minutes)

Use the Discipleship Pathway Planning Template to:

1. Define your discipleship destination (what maturity looks like in your context).
2. Identify stages of growth in your church.
3. Determine key milestones (be/know/do) for each stage.
4. Map your ministries to the pathway.
5. Assign leaders responsible for each stage.
6. Create a 90-day action plan to strengthen or launch your pathway.

 **LET'S REFLECT ... LET'S TALK**

Individual Reflection Questions – LEAD

1. Does my ministry have a clear plan to help people grow in faith?

2. How will I personally invest in at least one new leader this year?

3. What's one thing I can start doing immediately to multiply leaders?

Team Discussion Questions – LEAD

1. Which stage in our discipleship pathway is the weakest right now?

2. How can we better communicate our discipleship process to the congregation?

3. How will we measure growth in discipleship, not just attendance?

Suggested Tools & Resources

- Discipleship Pathway Planning Template (RPG Resource)

- The Master Plan of Evangelism by Robert Coleman

- Building a Discipling Culture by Mike Breen

- Volunteer Onboarding Checklist (RPG Resource)

- Leadership Pipeline Diagram (RPG Resource)

NOTE: Scan the QR code on page 111 to download the RPG templates.

2.4 – L.E.A.D.S.S. In Action

Personal Engagement (Required Activities)

1. Complete your full Discipleship Pathway Planning Template.

2. Choose one apprentice and create a 60-day mentoring plan based on their needs.

3. Meet with your ministry team to review your leadership pipeline and identify 2-3 improvement areas.

4. Be ready to present a 2-minute overview of your discipleship pathway in the next session.

Group Engagement (Optional Activities if Available)

1. Share your ministry team's feedback to question #3 above on the group portal within 10 days for peer input.

2. Join a 30-minute group coaching call and note three key takeaways.

End Notes

Session 2 - Endnotes (Equip Disciples)

1. Robert E. Coleman, *The Master Plan of Evangelism* (Revell, 2010.)

2. Key Scripture references cited in Session 2 include: Matthew 28:18-20; Matthew 4:19; Matthew 11:29; John 14:15; Luke 6:40; 2 Timothy 2:2; Ephesians 4:11-16; Acts 6:1-7; Colossians 1:28-29; Exodus 18:13-26; Titus 1:5; Hebrews 5:12-14; Matthew 20:26-28; John 13:1-17; Mark 10:44-45.

3. Concepts on leadership, discipleship and multiplication in this session were generally influenced by:

- Greg Ogden, *Transforming Discipleship* (Downers Grove, IL: IVP, 2003).
- John C. Maxwell, *Developing the Leader Within You 2.0* (Nashville, TN: HarperCollins Leadership, 2018).
- Mike Breen, *Building a Discipling Culture* (Pawleys Island, SC: 3DM Publishing, 2017).
- Robert Coleman, *The Master Plan of Evangelism* (Grand Rapids, MI: Revell, 2010).

My Notes

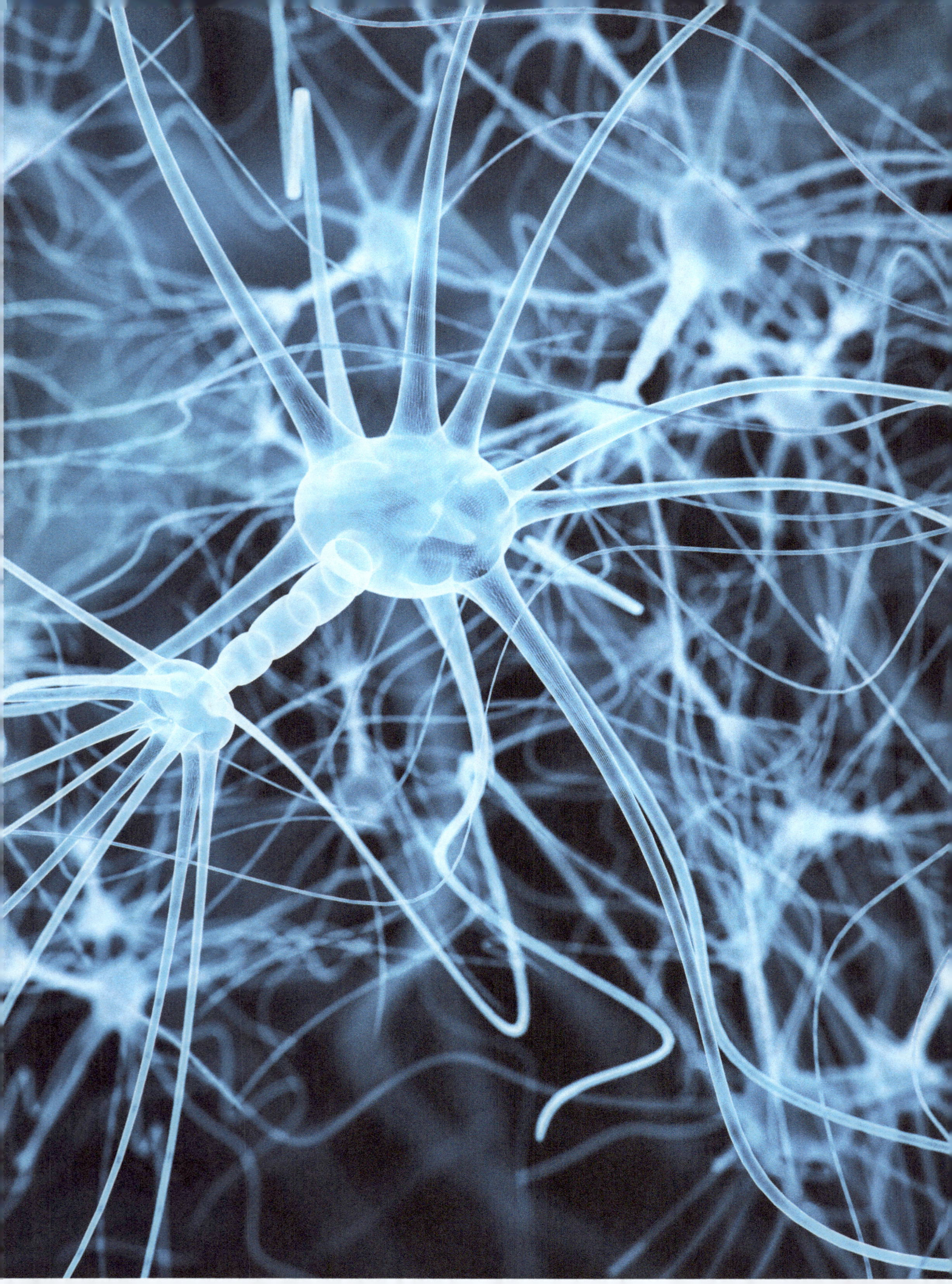

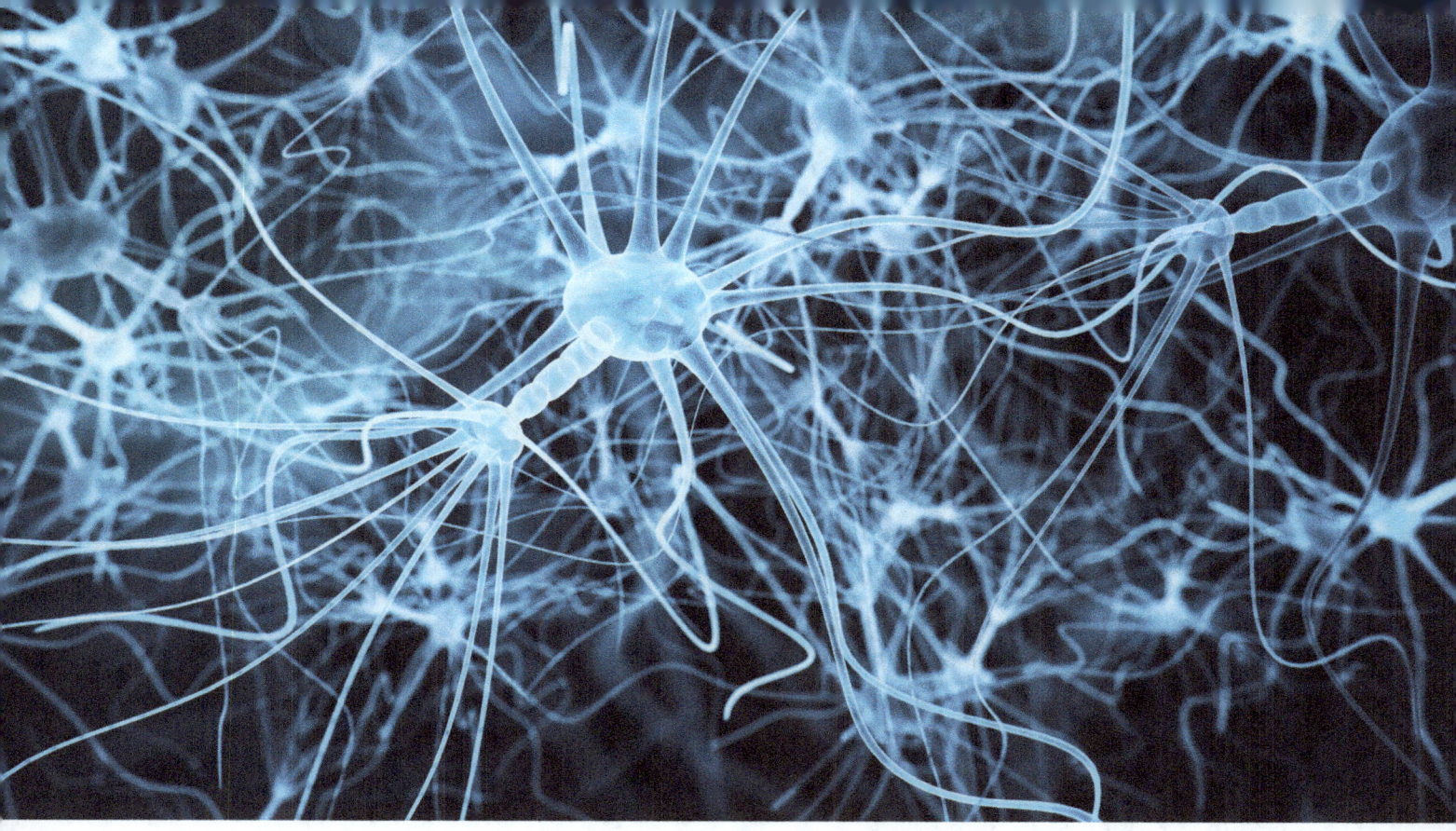

Session 3

ALIGN SYSTEMS

HEALTHY SYSTEMS THAT BUILD HEALTHY MINISTRIES
1 CORINTHIANS 3:6-8

Objective:

To help leaders build ministry systems that promote health, clarity, and sustainability. Participants will learn to audit existing processes, identify weak points, and implement streamlined systems that align structure with vision and strengthen overall ministry impact.

Session 2 Review – Equip Disciples

Before we move forward, let's revisit key concepts from Session Two to ensure our discipleship pathways and leader-equipping processes are ready to integrate into a healthy system.

Group Debrief (15-20 min)

1. **L.E.A.D.S.S. In Action Check-In and Peer Feedback (10 minutes)**

   - Briefly tell us about the 60-day mentoring plan that you developed with the apprentice your identified.
   - Share one way you have already seen your discipleship pathway strengthen ministry engagement.
   - Share one story of someone growing in leadership because of your intentional equipping.

2. **Peer Feedback (10 minutes)**

   - Present your discipleship pathway overview in 2 minutes.
   - Explain briefly 2 to 3 areas for improvement that you and your ministry team discovered you need to make with your current leadership pipeline.
   - Share 2-3 key reflections from a 30-minute coaching call that you attended.

Session 2 Summary

Session Two helped us equip people to carry the vision forward. Now, in Session Three, we will focus on aligning the systems that will support those people and keep the ministry healthy as it grows.

03

 ## 3.0 – Introduction

A system is a structured and repeatable process that helps people, ministries, or organizations function consistently and effectively. It provides clarity, order, and direction so that goals can be carried out in predictable ways, even by different people or over time.

Healthy systems don't replace the work of the Holy Spirit. Instead, they create space for the Spirit to move. On the one hand, without systems, vision fades and discipleship stalls. On the other, when systems become overly complex, leaders burn out and lose focus. The Bible shows that God values order and structure in His work.

God is a God of order, structure, and intentional design. From creation to the Early Church, we see that when God builds, He builds with clarity, roles, flow, and purpose (Genesis 1:1-31). In our churches, it is important to remember that ministry systems are not man-made inventions; they are biblical tools to support God's mission and people.

In Acts 6:1-7, the apostles established a structure to ensure needs were met and the mission continued. The result? Care increased, leaders multiplied, and the Word spread. Systems amplify ministry impact when they free pastors to shepherd, people to serve, and the Gospel to advance. Dr. A. Louis Patterson taught that when a church's order supports both the pastor's calling and the discipleship of its people, the church is equipped to accomplish God's divine purpose.[1]

Let's look at a few concepts that support this premise:

- Creation followed an intentional sequence (Genesis 1 - 2).
- Moses was given a clear organizational structure for leading Israel (Exodus 18:13-26).
- Jesus modeled simplicity in His ministry structure, small teams, clear instructions, and reproducible practices (Matthew - John).
- The Early Church had systems to ensure fairness and meet needs (Acts 6:1-7), promote shared leadership (Titus 1:5), and organize communication (Acts 15).

03

When systems align with the mission, they amplify the ministry's impact. When they don't, they create confusion, waste resources, and burn out leaders. In this session, you will learn how to assess your current ministry systems, identify bottlenecks, and align your structures with your vision and discipleship pathway.

Biblical Story Highlight – Systems Thinking

Let's look at Paul's words to the Corinthians. Read 1 Corinthians 3:6-8, and identify the distinct roles, shared mission, aligned efforts, and dependency on God's power that Paul describes in God's process of growth. Reflect on how each role, planting, watering, and increasing, relates to the systems and teamwork needed for a healthy church. After you have noted your observations, we will share insights as a group.

-
-
-
-

In 1 Corinthians 3:6-8, Paul reminds us that every role matters, but true fruitfulness depends on divine alignment, leaders working together under God's direction. When a church's systems, people, and ministries align with God's purpose, growth becomes both natural and sustainable.

 ## 3.1 – LEARN: Why Systems Matter in Ministry

Introduction to LEARN

In this section, we will explore how God uses order and structure in leadership to create healthy teams, guide His people, and advance His redemptive mission.

Key Scriptures & Insights with Practical Tips

Let's begin by taking time to review some key scriptures and foundational insights that will assist you in aligning your systems.

1. **Our God is a God of Order – Genesis 1:1 - 2:3**

   God created everything with intentional purpose and with perfect detail. His divine order brought peace, clarity, distinction, and direction, revealing His character and sustaining His creation. In ministry, we should seek to model God's orderly pattern as seen in Genesis 1:1 - 2:3, because order in leadership mirrors God's nature, and strengthens the health and unity of the church.[2]

   - **Cross References:** Jeremiah 31:35; Deuteronomy 27:10; Proverbs 16:3; Exodus 18:21-26; Numbers 11:16-17

   - **Practical Tip:** Write down every ministry process you currently have in place (*e.g., volunteer scheduling, small group placement, yearly ministry planning, etc.*). Afterwards, look through each of them and determine if the processes are clear, consistent, and simple. Later, have a few of your team members give you feedback as well.

2. **Systems Support Growth & the Mission – Acts 6:1-7**

   Healthy systems create structure that allow ministries to grow without losing focus. They keep people organized, vision clear, and resources aligned so the mission can move forward effectively and sustainably. In Acts 6:1-7, the apostles established a care system for widows, that utilized the service of what we know today as the first "Deacon Prototypes." This allowed the apostles to focus on teaching and prayer, the Gospel mission to spread, and the Church to continue flourishing.[3]

   - **Cross References: Nehemiah 4:13-23; Exodus 18:13-26**

   - **Practical Tip:** Take time to identify any recurring problems in your ministry and proactively create a repeatable process to prevent them.

3. **Alignment Prevents Mission Drift – Amos 3:3**

   Just as proper car alignment ensures a smoother ride and longer tire life, a church's vision thrives when it's actions and systems move in the same direction. Every ministry must work in unity to fulfill God's mission, because alignment strengthens the whole Body for lasting impact.[4] The connected appeal in Amos 3:3 further proves that relationships require a shared purpose, passion, and path, without which, the fulfillment of the mission will be elusive.

   - **Cross References:** Ecclesiastes 4:9-12; 1 Corinthians 3:6-8

   - **Practical Tip:** Review every ministry activity that you have on your yearly calendar, and every person that's leading it. Determine if the people leading and the activities themselves directly help fulfill your mission. If not, then it's time for a reset.

4. **Delegation Requires Structure – Titus 1:5**

   Effective delegation doesn't happen by accident; it needs clear organization. When leaders assign responsibilities with structure and support, others can serve confidently, and the ministry can grow in strength and order. In Titus 1:5, Paul instructed Titus to "set in order" the things left unfinished and appoint leaders. The instructions were clear, coordinated, and carried out appropriately.

03

- **Cross References:** Mark 6:39-40; Luke 10:1-9; Exodus 18:13-26; 35-39

- **Practical Tip:** Create an Org Chart for your ministry, and share it with your team. It is important to note that clarity of roles increases ownership and reduces burnout.

 **LET'S REFLECT ... LET'S TALK**

Individual Reflection Questions – LEARN

1. Where do I see a lack of structure slowing down our ministry?

2. Which system in my ministry is the most effective right now? Why?

3. Do I have clarity on who is responsible for each major ministry function?

Team Discussion Questions – LEARN

1. Which ministry area causes the most "reactive firefighting" instead of proactive leadership?

2. Are our current systems simple enough for anyone to follow?

3. How well do our systems reflect our mission and discipleship pathway?

3.2 – LINK: Assessing & Aligning Our Current Systems

Introduction to LINK

In this section, you will apply the biblical principles we have studied to evaluate your church's current systems. Take time to assess, discuss, and make necessary adjustments that lead to better alignment with God's mission. Use the notes and insights you developed in the 3.1 Practical Tips section to guide your review and next steps.

Classroom Contextualization Process

Let's take a practical look at how your church's systems currently function, and identify where improvement is needed for greater clarity, unity, and mission alignment. This process moves us from understanding the importance of systems to actively strengthening them in real time.

 Step 1 – Ministry Systems Inventory (10 min)

Objective: Identify and organize all existing ministry systems to gain a clear picture of how your church currently operates.

- Write down every recurring process (*e.g., visitor follow-up, volunteer recruitment, budgeting, event planning*).

- Group them into these categories: Outreach, Discipleship, Care, and Administration. (**Note:** *You may use these four general groupings, or others more suitable for your church's context.*)

Step 2 – Identify Bottlenecks (10 min)

Objective: Recognize areas where processes slow down or create frustration so you can remove barriers to ministry effectiveness.

- Where do tasks get stuck?

- What takes longer than it should?

- Which processes cause frustration for leaders or members?

Step 3 – Check Mission Alignment (15 min)

Objective: Evaluate whether each system supports the church's mission, simplifies ministry, and empowers leaders to focus on discipleship.

- For each system, ask:

  ▷ Does it support our mission and discipleship pathway?

  ▷ Is it simple enough to be reproduced?

  ▷ Does it free up leaders for ministry, or weigh them down?

Step 4 – Check Mission Alignment (15 min)

Objective: Select key systems to strengthen in the next 90 days, focusing on changes that will create the greatest immediate Kingdom impact.

- Pick 1-2 systems to improve over the next 90 days.
- Decide what changes will have the biggest Kingdom impact right now.

 **LET'S REFLECT ... LET'S TALK**

Individual Reflection Questions – LINK

1. Which of my ministry's systems frustrates me most?

2. Which system most excites me because of its impact?

3. What's one small change I could make to improve a process this month?

Team Discussion Questions – LINK

1. Which of our current systems are most in need of a redesign?

2. Do our leaders understand and use our systems consistently?

3. How could simplifying our systems release more energy for ministry?

3.3 – LEAD: Creating Systems that Serve the Mission

Introduction to LEAD

In this section, we will design or refine systems that help the ministry run smoothly while keeping the mission at its core. We will do this through a Systems Audit Workshop.

Workshop Activity – Systems Audit Template (35-40 minutes)

The System Audit Template helps church leaders evaluate, simplify, and align ministry systems so they serve the mission, support discipleship, and empower leaders.

NOTE: *A system is any repeatable process your ministry uses to accomplish a task, from visitor follow-up to small group leader training to budget approvals.*

Systems Audit Template (Exercise)

- Using the System Audit Template, pick 1-2 key systems in your church to audit (*Complete instructions for this exercise are located on the template*).
- When you are finished, share your findings with your peers for input.
- Also, list at least two improvements that you and your team can implement in the next 90 days.

 **LET'S REFLECT … LET'S TALK**

Individual Reflection Questions – LEAD

1. What's one system I will improve this month?

2. How will I communicate these changes to my team?

3. How will I measure if the system is improved after making the changes?

Team Discussion Questions – LINK

1. Which system improvement will have the fastest ministry impact?

2. Who needs to be trained on the new process?

3. How will we ensure the system stays simple and effective over time?

Suggested Tools & Resources

- Systems Audit Template (RPG Resource)

- Simple Church by Thom Rainer & Eric Geiger

- Deliberate Simplicity by Dave Browning

- Flowchart & Process Mapping Tools (Lucidchart, Miro, or even whiteboards)

NOTE: Scan the QR code on page 111 to download the RPG templates.

 ## 3.4 – L.E.A.D.S.S. In Action

Personal Engagement (Required Activities)

1. Complete a Systems Audit for two additional ministry systems.
2. Implement one improvement from your audit before Session Four and be ready to share your "Before & After" update.

Group Engagement (Optional Activities if Available)

1. Share one example of a healthy leader or leadership team on the group portal within 10 days for peer feedback.
2. Join a 30-minute group coaching call and note three key takeaways.

End Notes

Session 3 - Endnotes (Align Systems)

1. Patterson, A. Louis. (Sermons & Lessons)
2. Sanders, J. Oswald. Spiritual Leadership. Moody Publishers, 2007.
3. Blackaby, Henry, and Richard Blackaby. Spiritual Leadership: Moving People on to God's Agenda. B&H Publishing, 2011.
4. Lencioni, Patrick. The Advantage: Why Organizational Health Trumps Everything Else in Business.
5. Key Scripture references cited in Session 3 include: Genesis 1 - 2; Acts 6:1-7; Nehemiah 4:13-23; Exodus 18:13-26; Amos 3:3; Ecclesiastes 4:9-12; 1 Corinthians 3:6-8; Titus 1:5; Mark 6:39-40; Luke 10:1-9; Numbers 11:16-17.
6. Conceptual influence on ministry alignment, leadership pipelines, clarity, systems, healthy organizational culture, and simplicity concepts in this session were generally influenced by:

   - Aubrey Malphurs, *Developing Leaders for the 21st Century*. Grand Rapids, MI: Baker Books, 1999.
   - Dave Browning, *Deliberate Simplicity* (Grand Rapids, MI: Zondervan, 2009).
   - Patrick Lencioni, *The Advantage* (San Francisco, CA: Jossey-Bass, 2012).
   - Thom Rainer & Eric Geiger, *Simple Church* (Nashville, TN: B&H Publishing, 2006).
   - Tony Evans, *Kingdom Focused Church* (Chicago, IL: Moody Publishers, 2003).

My Notes

Session 4

DESIGN FOR GROWTH

CREATING PATHWAYS FOR SPIRITUAL MATURITY
COLOSSIANS 1:28-29

Objective:

To guide leaders in creating intentional pathways that move people from conversion to maturity. Participants will design a clear discipleship map for their church or ministry that connects teaching, relationships, and service opportunities for holistic spiritual formation.

04   Session 4

DESIGN FOR GROWTH
CREATING PATHWAYS FOR SPIRITUAL GROWTH
COLOSSIANS 1:28-29

 Session 3 Review – Align Systems

Before shifting our focus toward discipleship growth, we must ensure that the systems we built in our previous sessions are functioning well enough to support it. A discipleship plan is only as strong as the systems that deliver it.

Group Debrief (15-20 min)

1. **L.E.A.D.S.S. In Action Check-In and Peer Feedback (10 minutes)**
   - Briefly share one completed audited system and the changes you made.
   - Share one specific way your improved system has made ministry smoother or more impactful.
   - Share a bottleneck that was removed and how it freed you or your team to focus on people.

2. **Peer Feedback (10 minutes)**
   - Present one audited system and the changes you made, and receive 2-3 practical suggestions from the group for further improvement.

Session 3 Summary

Session Three's focus on Aligning Systems was about building healthy ministry structures. Today's session is about ensuring those structures exist to grow people, not just to manage programs. Remember, God has not called us to the business of "running events." We are called instead to the ministry of "making disciples."

 ## 4.0 – Introduction

Discipleship is not just the start of the Christian journey; it is the intentional lifelong process of becoming more like Jesus, and helping others do the same. Designing for growth means creating intentional pathways that help people mature spiritually. It is the process of building clear steps, environments, and support systems that guide believers from where they are, to where God wants them to be. The goal of discipling for growth is maturity in Christ, not mere attendance or program completion.

In Colossians 1:28, the Apostle Paul described his mission this way:

> *"We proclaim Him, admonishing every man and teaching every man with all wisdom, so that we may present every man complete in Christ."*

Biblical discipleship is intentional, relational, and transformational. It calls for a clear plan that helps believers grow in faith, character, and service. Without such a pathway, people often plateau or drift in their spiritual journey.

Jesus didn't just invite people to believe in Him, He called them to follow Him and become like Him. True discipleship is not about gaining more information, but about experiencing genuine transformation. In reflecting on the importance of discipleship, Dawson Trotman, founder of The Navigators, once stated:

> *"Discipleship that forms only minds produces spectators, but discipleship that forms lives produces multipliers."* **– Dawson Trotman**[1]

Simply put, God has called us to teach for "transformation," and not just for "information." In this session, you will:

- Define what spiritual maturity looks like in your context.
- Identify the stages of growth in your church.
- Design a Discipleship Growth Plan that leaders can implement immediately.

Biblical Story Highlight – Growing Intentionally

Let's turn to Paul's letter to the Colossians. Read Colossians 1:28-29, and identify Paul's goal for every believer, and the process he describes for achieving it. Next to the bullet points below, note how his stated goals, along with God's power offer, a solid framework to how we should design and grow our ministries. Once you have completed this exercise, we will discuss your observations together.

-
-
-
-

In Colossians 1:28-29, Paul shows that true growth comes from intentional discipleship, teaching, warning, and laboring to present every believer mature in Christ. Growth doesn't happen by accident, and when leaders partner with God's strength and build systems that mature disciples, the church grows in both depth and impact.

Jesus as the Master Teacher

We will talk more about this pattern in Session Six, but today, let's take a look at Jesus' intentional discipleship plan. It involves six major areas:

- **Enlisting:** He invited them to come follow Him (Matthew 4:18-22; Mark 1:16-20; Luke 5:2-11; John 1:40-43).
- **Equipping:** He invested in a few and taught them God's truth (Mark 3:14-15; Matthew 5-7; 16:24-27).
- **Emulating:** He showed them how to live (John 13:15; Mark 10:44-45; 1 Peter 5:3).
- **Engaging:** He allowed them to participate in serving others (Matthew 15:29-39; Luke 10:1-9; John 6:1-15).

- **Encouraging:** He prayed for their unity and mission, and taught them how to pray while on mission (John 17:20-23; Matthew 6:9-15; 26:36-36; Luke 11:1-13; 22:40-46).
- **Empowering:** He commissioned and sent them out with authority to represent His Kingdom and minister to others, while promising the Spirit's presence and power with them (Luke 9:1-6; 10:1-9; Matthew 10:1-42; 28:18-20; Acts 1:8).

So how does Jesus' model relate to church-designed discipleship growth systems? This means churches must begin creating intentional pathways that:

1. Help people start their faith or mentoring journey.
2. Guide people into healthy habits and community.
3. Encourage and equip people to serve others and lead daily.
4. Release people to multiply disciples.

04

 ## 4.1 – LEARN: The Biblical Call to Spiritual Growth

Introduction to LEARN

This section is about grounding ourselves in God's definition of spiritual maturity. Many churches have activities, but activities are not the same as growth. In this section, we will look at Scripture to define what growth looks like and how it's measured biblically.

Key Scriptures & Insights with Practical Tips

Let's begin by taking time to review some key scriptures and foundational insights that will assist you in creating pathways for spiritual growth.

1. **Growth is God's Will – Colossians 1:28-29**

    To accomplish the Kingdom goals He has for us, God desires every believer to mature in faith and purpose. In God's economy, maturity means stability, discernment, and Christlike character. When we grow spiritually, we reflect God's will for us to become more like Christ, as we use our strength and His power to help others grow in Christ. In Colossians 1:28-29, Paul's mission was to strive with every fiber of his being to present everyone "mature in Christ." This is a mission we are encouraged to imitate.

    - **Cross References:** Ephesians 4:13-15; 2 Timothy 3:17; 1 Peter 2:2; Romans 1:11-17

    - **Practical Tip:** Write a one-sentence definition of maturity for your church, so everyone is aiming at the same target.

2. **Spiritual Growth is Intentional – 2 Peter 1:5-11**

    Growing in faith does not happen by accident, but requires intentional commitment, discipline, and time with God (*e.g., prayer, study, obedience, community, etc.*). These practices shape us to reflect Christ daily. Peter reminds us of this disciplined growth mindset in 2 Peter 1:5-11.

04

- **Cross References:** Hebrews 5:12-14; Galatians 5; 1 Timothy 4:11-16; 2 Timothy 2:22; 3:14-17

- **Practical Tip:** Create a "next step checklist" for your congregation that outlines a simple action they can take to grow spiritually, regardless of where they are in their journey.

3. **Growth Happens in Community – Acts 2:42-47**

Spiritual growth thrives in relationships. We mature best when we learn, serve, and grow alongside others. This shared sense of presence serves as a catalyst to encourage, challenge, and support us in living out our faith. In Acts 2:42-47, the early disciples exercised these principles, and grew together through teaching, fellowship, breaking bread, and prayer.

- **Cross References:** Proverbs 27:17; Psalm 133; Acts 17:11-21

- **Practical Tip:** Begin thinking about a system your church can implement to make small groups, mentoring, or accountability relationships a non-negotiable part of your growth plan.

4. **Growth Produces Multiplication – 2 Timothy 2:2**

A natural sign of spiritual maturity is reproduction. As believers mature, they intentionally invest in others, helping new disciples grow in faith, and expand the Gospel's impact. In 2 Timothy 2:2, Paul gave Timothy a model for mature leadership, disciples who grow and reproduce themselves.

- **Cross References:** John 15:8; Luke 6:39-40; 1 Kings 19:19-21; 2 Kings 2:1-15

- **Practical Tip:** Incorporate leadership training into your discipleship process to ensure growth doesn't end with the individual, but continues through multiplication.

 **LET'S REFLECT ... LET'S TALK**

Individual Reflection Questions – LEARN

1. How do I currently define "spiritual maturity"?

2. Which Scripture most challenges my approach to discipleship?

3. Where am I personally still growing?

Team Discussion Questions – LEARN

1. Do we have a shared definition of maturity in our church?

2. Are we helping people take their next step, or just keeping them busy?

3. How are we multiplying disciple-makers?

 ## 4.2 – LINK: Evaluating Discipleship in Our Context

Introduction to LINK

In this section, you will apply what you have learned to your actual ministry reality. So lean in, think critically, be honest, and remember that God desires for your ministry team to reproduce healthy leaders who reproduce healthy leaders. This exercise is designed to help you achieve this goal.

Classroom Contextualization Process

This activity helps you draw out your current discipleship journey and identify where people are growing and where they tend to stop progressing. By seeing the pathway clearly, you can strengthen strong areas and address the gaps that hinder disciple-making.

Instructions:
- Map out your current discipleship process, from first-time guest to mature disciple-maker. Identify where people are thriving by circling those stages, and mark with a red X the areas where individuals seem to get "stuck."
- Once your map is complete, share it with others at your table or another group to receive feedback and new ideas for strengthening your discipleship pathway.
- Use Steps 1-4 below for additional support on creating your map.

 ### Step 1 – Discipleship Pathway Map Review (10 min)

- Draw out your church's process on paper or a whiteboard.

 ### Step 2 – Identify Growth Gaps (10 min)

- **Ask:** Where do people drop out? What's missing?

 Step 3 – Evaluate Balance (15 min)

- Is there a balance of teaching, community, serving, and sending?

 Step 4 – Connect to Systems (15 min)

- Link Session 3 systems to your discipleship steps to ensure each one is supported.

 # LET'S REFLECT ... LET'S TALK

Individual Reflection Questions – LINK

1. Do we know clearly where our people are in their spiritual growth journey?

2. What's the weakest stage in our pathway?

3. Are our systems actually helping people grow, or just keeping things organized?

Team Discussion Questions – LINK

1. Which steps could be clearer or simpler?

2. Are we over-relying on events instead of relationships?

3. Who is an example of the maturity we want to multiply?

4.3 – LEAD: Designing a Discipleship Growth Plan

Introduction to LEAD

By the end of this session, you will have a draft discipleship growth plan uniquely designed for your church. This plan will serve as a practical tool to strengthen both your personal and collective approach to making and maturing disciples.

Workshop Activity – Discipleship Growth Plan Template

The Discipleship Growth Plan Template provides a clear, step-by-step pathway to help believers grow from spiritual infancy to maturity. It outlines intentional stages, environments, and leadership support designed to guide and strengthen each disciple's journey.

Best Practices for Using the Plan

- **Make it Simple** – Don't overcomplicate with too many stages. Start with 3-5.
- **Make it Visual** – Display your professionally designed pathway on quality stationery throughout your church and media outlets.
- **Make it Repetitive** – Create a simple graphic and share it in New Members' classes, leadership meetings, volunteer trainings, etc.
- **Make it Measurable** – Use the indicators to celebrate growth and identify where someone needs more support.
- **Make it Ministry Integrated** – Ensure every ministry within your church understands, integrates, and consistently shares the pathway.

NOTE: *If your church already has a discipleship "philosophy" but not a clear "pathway," this template will turn your ideas into a concrete, reproducible process.*

Instructions:

- Use the Discipleship Growth Plan Template to complete at least two stages of your pathway during this workshop (*Complete instructions for this exercise are located on the template*).
- Share your draft with your table for immediate feedback.
- Share and complete your growth plan with your lead team.

 # LET'S REFLECT ... LET'S TALK

Individual Reflection Questions – LEAD

1. How will I personally model growth?

2. Which stage will I focus on first?

3. How will I measure actual growth, not just activity?

Team Discussion Questions – LINK

1. How can we integrate this into every ministry?

2. Who will lead implementation?

3. How will we celebrate progress?

Suggested Tools & Resources

- Discipleship Growth Plan Template (RPG Resource)

- Transforming Discipleship by Greg Ogden

- Discipleshift by Jim Putman

- Bible reading plans

- Spiritual Gifts Assessments

NOTE: Scan the QR code on page 111 to download the RPG templates.

 ## 4.4 – L.E.A.D.S.S. In Action

Personal Engagement (Required Activities)

1. Complete your full Discipleship Growth Plan.

2. Identify two people to invest in over the next 90 days.

3. Prepare to present key highlights in Session Five.

Group Engagement (Optional Activities if Available)

1. Share one strategy for helping ministry leaders align their ministries with the pathway on the group portal within 10 days.

2. Join a 30-minute group coaching call and note three key takeaways.

End Notes

Session 4 - Endnotes (Design For Growth)

1. Dawson Trotman, *Born to Reproduce* (Colorado Springs, CO: NavPress, 1955).

2. Key Scripture references cited in Session 4 include: Colossians 1:28-29; Matthew 4:18-22; Mark 3:14-15; John 13:15; Luke 10:1-9; Matthew 5 - 7; 2 Peter 1:5-11; Hebrews 5:12-14; Galatians 5; Acts 2:42-47; John 15:8; Luke 6:39-40.

3. Leadership and multiplication concepts, discipleship pathways & spiritual growth concepts in this session were generally influenced by:

- Alan Hirsch, *The Forgotten Ways: Reactivating the Missional Church*. Grand Rapids, MI: Brazos Press, 2016.

- Aubrey Malphurs, *Developing a Discipleship Strategy: A Systems Approach to Ministry*. Grand Rapids, MI: Baker Books, 1999.

- Colin Marshall & Tony Payne, *The Vine Project* (Kingsford, Australia: Matthias Media, 2016).

- Dallas Willard, *The Divine Conspiracy* (San Francisco, CA: HarperCollins, 1998).

- Donald Whitney, *Spiritual Disciplines for the Christian Life* (Colorado Springs, CO: NavPress, 2014).

- Eric Geiger, *Transformational Discipleship* (Nashville, TN: B&H Publishing, 2012).

My Notes

Session 5

SERVE THE WORLD
DEVELOPING A MISSIONAL MINDSET
JOHN 20:19-21

Objective:

To inspire leaders with biblical truths to help them cultivate a missional culture that extends the Gospel beyond church walls. Participants will explore biblical models of mission, assess their local context, and create a Community Impact Strategy that mobilizes members to live missionally in every sphere of life.

05

 ## Session 4 Review – Design For Growth

We begin this session by ensuring that the discipleship growth plans you developed in Session Four are being implemented, not just written down. Remember, the goal is to ensure that every believer in your church is moving toward maturity and multiplication.

Group Debrief (15-20 min)

1. **L.E.A.D.S.S. In Action Check-In and Peer Feedback (10 minutes)**

   - Briefly share any discoveries or challenges concerning your Discipleship Growth Plan.
   - Briefly share details about your initial meeting with the 2 people you identified to invest in over the next 90 days.
   - Share one breakthrough in clarifying your church's pathway.

2. **Peer Feedback (10 minutes)**

   - Share one stage of your growth plan and your "next step" strategy, and receive 2-3 practical suggestions from the group to strengthen it.

Session 4 Summary

We have focused on growing disciples inside the church in Session Four. Now, we will focus on mobilizing those disciples to make an impact outside the church in their neighborhoods, workplaces, cities, and throughout the world.

05

 ## 5.0 – Introduction

The church is not just a building we visit, but both a family to belong to, and an army sent with a purpose to fulfill God's mission (John 20:21). Serving the world means living out the mission of Jesus beyond the church walls by meeting needs, building relationships, and sharing the Gospel locally and globally. It reflects God's heart for people and sends disciples as everyday missionaries.

For disciples, serving the world is not optional, but is the natural overflow of spiritual maturity and of knowing Jesus. In the Early Church, there was no separation between "discipleship" and "mission." The believers understood that commitment to following Jesus meant joining Him in His mission to seek and save the lost (Luke 19:10).

In his book *Multiply: Disciples Making Disciples*, Francis Chan explains it this way:

> *"An inwardly focused church is an unhealthy church. Biblically, a church that fails to look at the world around it is no church at all."* – Francis Chan[1]

In this session, we will shift our focus from inside-the-walls growth to outside-the-walls impact. Our goal is not just to run programs that meet needs internally, but to mobilize disciples who see service and mission as part of their everyday lives externally.

Biblical Story Highlight – Serving Intentionally

Take a moment to read John 20:19-21. Note the key words or phrases below that Jesus uses as instructions or commissions to His disciples. After completing your notes, we will come together to discuss your insights and reflections.

-
-
-
-

In John 20:19-21, Jesus appears to His disciples, bringing peace and purpose, and sends them out just as the Father sent Him. This passage should remind us that every Christ follower is called and empowered to continue His mission in the world.

05

 ## 5.1 – LEARN: The Biblical Mandate to Serve and Go

Introduction to LEARN

If discipleship is about becoming like Jesus, then service is about doing what Jesus did. We are sent into the world not just to help people, but to point them to the One who can save them. Most importantly, serving the world is not about adding another program, but about embedding a missional mindset in every believer.

Key Scriptures & Insights with Practical Tips

Let's begin by taking time to review some key scriptures and foundational insights that will assist your church in serving the world.

1. **Serving is Following Jesus – Mark 10:45**

   To serve others reflects the heart of Christ, is an act of love, and is a fruit of discipleship. Jesus came not to be served, but to serve and give His life away to others. In Mark 10:45, Jesus made this perfectly clear to His disciples, and as His followers, He expects us to model His example.

   - **Cross References:** Mark 2:1-12; Luke 7:1-10; John 6:5-14; Philippians 2:5-8

   - **Practical Tip:** Regularly highlight servant stories in your church and on your media platforms so people see service not as the exception, but as the norm.

2. **We Are All Sent – Matthew 28:18-20**

   Sadly, over the years, many Christians have falsely believed that only a select few are called and commissioned to represent Jesus in the world. In Matthew 28:18-20, Jesus commissions His disciples to make disciples of all nations, baptizing and teaching them to obey His commands. This same call extends to us today; we are all sent to share the Gospel, multiply disciples, and carry Christ's presence and authority into every part of the world.

- **Cross References:** Matthew 24:14; Mark 16:15; John 20:21; Acts 1:8; 13:47; 26:14-18

- **Practical Tip:** Train and challenge every believer to identify their "mission field" (*e.g., home, work, community*) and to serve the people there faithfully.

3. **Service is a Witness – Matthew 5:14-16**

   When we serve others intentionally with love and respect, and live a life that is transparent and truthful, our good works glorify God and point people to Him. In Matthew 5:14-16, Jesus affirms this truth to His disciples, and it serves as a reminder for us to let our good deeds be seen so God is honored.

   - **Cross References:** Ephesians 2:10; Philippians 2:12-15; Titus 3:14; 1 Peter 2:11-15; 3:15-17

   - **Practical Tip:** Teach disciples in your church how to suffer well, and how to pair every service activity with relational follow-up and Gospel conversations.

4. **Mission is Local and Global – Acts 1:8**

   God's global mission starts in our homes, but it does not stop there. Christ's commission to share the Gospel extends to the ends of the earth. In His final message before ascending into heaven in Acts 1:8, Jesus set this expectation for all of His followers.

   - **Cross References:** Acts 13:1-5; Romans 1:16; 10:14-15; Matthew 10:7-8

   - **Practical Tip:** In your yearly calendar, create rhythms that include both local outreach and global mission opportunities for your members.

 # LET'S REFLECT ... LET'S TALK

Individual Reflection Questions – LEARN

1. How do I personally live out my call to serve others?

2. Where is my primary mission field at the moment?

3. What fears or obstacles hold me back from serving?

Team Discussion Questions – LEARN

1. How well is our church modeling service as a lifestyle?

2. Are we more focused on in-house ministry than outreach?

3. What stories of impact can we share to inspire others?

5.2 – LINK: Evaluating Our Church's Engagement

Introduction to LINK

In the LEARN section, we saw God's call to serve. Now in the LINK section, we will bring that call into our unique ministry contexts. This is where you will begin assessing if you are actually doing what God commanded and commissioned us to do.

Many churches do great things in outreach, but they often lack a clear strategy, which means they can be busy without being effective. LINK helps us slow down and:

- Identify what we're doing well.
- Spot where we are missing opportunities.
- Measure whether our service is actually making disciples.

The truth is, not all outreach is equally fruitful. We want to invest our energy where it has the greatest impact on the Kingdom. This means we must evaluate both our local and global efforts to ensure they align with our discipleship pathway, as outlined in Session Four.

Classroom Contextualization Process

This activity helps leaders connect biblical truth to practical action by evaluating how well their church engages its community and fulfills Christ's mission. This reflection fosters clarity, alignment, and next steps for greater Kingdom impact.

Instructions:

- Brainstorm your church's current outreach and mission activities. List every outreach and mission effort your church is currently involved in, and note whether it's ongoing or a one-time event.
- Next, evaluate each event for relational depth and Gospel impact. Finally, identify any gaps you discover and discuss ways to close them.
- Use Steps 1-4 below as an additional guide to complete this exercise.

 Step 1 – Outreach & Mission Inventory (10 min)

- List all current local and global mission activities.

 Step 2 – Impact Evaluation (15 min)

For each activity, discuss:

- Does this meet a real need?
- Does it open doors for the Gospel?
- Are people being discipled through serving?

 Step 3 – Engagement Gaps (10 min)

- Where are we not present but should be?
- Which needs are going unmet?

 Step 4 – Integration with Discipleship (15 min)

- How can serving real needs be tied to our discipleship growth plan from Session Four?

 **LET'S REFLECT ... LET'S TALK**

Individual Reflection Questions – LINK

1. Which outreach effort am I most passionate about?

2. Where do I see the biggest gap in our outreach/community engagement?

3. How could I personally bridge that gap?

Team Discussion Questions – LINK

1. Which current outreach has the deepest relational impact?

2. What would it take to double our engagement in the next year?

3. How can we better connect service to disciple-making?

5.3 – LEAD: Building an Outreach Engagement Plan

Introduction to LEAD

Too often, churches do random acts of kindness or occasional mission trips without a clear follow-up plan. The Outreach Engagement Plan brings focus and structure to your ministry by clarifying purpose, defining leadership and timelines, and ensuring every outreach effort leads to deeper, Gospel-centered discipleship.

Whether a local food drive or a global mission trip, this template will ensure that your event has:

- A clear purpose.

- A defined target group.

- Specific action steps.

- A leader assigned.

- A Gospel connection.

- A follow-up strategy to integrate people into the life of the church.

Remember, the goal is not about "just doing good things," but it is about advancing God's Kingdom with skill and in excellence.

Workshop Activity – Discipleship Growth Plan Template

Use this template alongside your Discipleship Growth Plan from Session Four to ensure outreach efforts naturally lead to discipleship. For example, when someone accepts Christ during a community event, you will already have a clear pathway for their spiritual growth and maturity in place.

Best Practices for Using the Plan

- **Always Assign a Passionate Leader –** Every project needs clear ownership and capable leadership. Even great plans fail without it.
- **Always Keep the Gospel Central –** Good works must point to the Good News, otherwise, the mission loses its purpose.
- **Always Plan Follow-Up First –** Prepare to connect and disciple before you begin. Outreach without follow-up wastes opportunity.
- **Always Celebrate Wins –** Share stories of God's work to inspire faith and keep momentum strong.
- **Always Review and Adjust –** Evaluate every effort and refine your approach for greater impact next time.

Instructions:

- Choose at least one local and one global initiative to develop. Use the Outreach Engagement Plan Template to define the purpose, steps, and leaders (*Complete instructions for this exercise are located on the template*).
- Next, share your draft with your table for input and ideas.

By the end of LEAD, you will walk away with a tangible, ready-to-implement plan to help your church serve the world more effectively.

How to Use the Template

Fill out one template for each outreach or mission initiative you want to host. It works for:

- Ongoing ministries (*e.g., monthly homeless outreach*)
- Seasonal events (*e.g., Christmas toy drive*)
- One-time projects (*e.g., disaster relief trip*)

To receive more feedback and support with completing this template, schedule brainstorming sessions with your team in leadership planning meetings, ministry team workshops, or small group missional brainstorming sessions.

05

 **LET'S REFLECT … LET'S TALK**

Individual Reflection Questions – LEAD

1. What's one outreach I will personally commit to this year?

2. Who will I invite to join me in serving?

3. How will I follow up with people I serve?

Team Discussion Questions – LINK

1. How can we increase participation in serving?

2. What's one new initiative we could launch this year?

3. How will we measure spiritual fruit, not just attendance?

> **Suggested Tools & Resources**
>
> - Outreach Engagement Plan Template (RPG Resource)
> - Serving Without Sinking by John Hindley
> - Community needs assessment tools
> - Short-term mission trip planning guides
>
> **NOTE:** Scan the QR code on page 111 to download the RPG templates.

 ## 5.4 – L.E.A.D.S.S. In Action

Personal Engagement (Required Activities)

1. Complete your Outreach Engagement Plan for one local and one global initiative.
2. Recruit and meet with your outreach team to review the plan.
3. Be ready to share your progress in the Session Six review.

Group Engagement (Optional Activities if Available)

1. Launch one step from your plan before Session Six and share the update on the group portal within 10 days for feedback.
2. Join a 30-minute group coaching call and note three key takeaways.

End Notes

Session 5 - Endnotes (Serve The World)

1. Francis Chan, *Multiply: Disciples Making Disciples* (Colorado Springs, CO: David C. Cook, 2012), 17.

2. Key Scripture references cited throughout Session 5 include: Mark 10:45; Luke 19:10; Matthew 5:14-16; Matthew 28:18-20; John 20:21; Acts 1:8; Acts 13:1-5; Romans 1:16; Titus 3:14.

3. Concepts on missional living, everyday missionary practices, and local/global engagement in this session were generally influenced by:

   - Alan Hirsch, *The Forgotten Ways* (Grand Rapids, MI: Brazos Press, 2016).
   - Eric Geiger & Thom Rainer, *Simple Church* (Nashville, TN: B&H Publishing, 2006).
   - Dave Browning, *Deliberate Simplicity* (Grand Rapids, MI: Zondervan, 2009).
   - John Perkins, *Let Justice Roll Down* (Grand Rapids, MI: Baker Books, 2010).
   - John Perkins, *One Blood* (Chicago, IL: Moody Publishers, 2018).
   - Tony Evans, *The Kingdom Agenda* (Chicago, IL: Moody Publishers, 2006).

My Notes

Session 6

SECURE THE FUTURE

BUILT BIBLICALLY FOR KINGDOM IMPACT
NUMBERS 27:18–20

Objective:

To equip leaders with the necessary tools to build sustainable ministries and future-ready teams. Participants will integrate all five pillars of clarity, discipleship, systems, growth, and mission, into a comprehensive Church Strengthening Plan. They will present their plans for peer review and receive feedback for refinement and implementation.

06 Session 6

SECURE THE FUTURE
BUILT BIBLICALLY FOR KINGDOM IMPACT
NUMBERS 27:18-20

 Session 5 Review – Serve the World

In our previous session, we learned that serving the world naturally flows from spiritual maturity. True disciples don't remain in classrooms; they instead move into their communities and the world to live and to share the love of Jesus. Discipleship is measured not by what we know, but by how we go and make Christ known. The real fruit of outreach is found not just in acts of service, but in building relationships, sharing the Gospel, and multiplying disciples.

Group Debrief (15-20 min)

1. **L.E.A.D.S.S. In Action Check-In and Peer Feedback (10 minutes)**
   - Briefly tell us about the step that you launched from your Outreach Engagement Plan, and what systems you established for follow-up.

2. **Sharing Wins**
   - Tell one story where an act of service created a Gospel or discipleship opportunity.

3. **Peer Feedback**
   - Share your most impactful outreach moment.
   - Receive 2-3 practical suggestions from peers to expand or refine your approach.

Session 5 Summary

The mission of the church is not complete when physical needs are met; it is complete when lives are transformed by Jesus. In Session Six, we will take the next step, building systems and developing leaders so that outreach, discipleship, and leadership multiply beyond us.

6.0 – Introduction

Secure the Future means building ministry strategies, systems, and leaders that ensure the mission continues with strength, clarity, and faithfulness long after current leaders are gone. Healthy churches don't just run programs—they build sustainable, Spirit-led structures that align people around a shared mission.

Over the past five sessions of L.E.A.D.S.S., you have developed essential tools: Vision Clarity, a Discipleship Pathway, Aligned Systems, a Discipleship Growth Plan, and an Outreach Engagement Plan. In this final session, we bring every principle together into one unified ministry framework. You will learn how to integrate vision, systems, discipleship, and mission into a cohesive plan that advances God's work today while securing long-term impact for generations to come.

The goal is to help you build a biblically grounded, transferable strategy that others can carry forward with excellence—even in your absence. Two powerful leadership truths capture the heart of this session:

> *"A ministry that dies when a leader leaves was never built on discipleship, it was built on personality…. Legacy leadership builds people who build people." – Dr. Myles Munroe*[1]

> *"A legacy is created only when a person puts his organization into the position to do great things without him." – Dr. John Maxwell*[2]

Biblical Story Highlight – A Secured Future

Take a moment to read Numbers 27:18-20. Next to the bullet points below, briefly list ways that Moses secured the future of Israel's leadership. After completing your notes, we will come together to discuss your insights and reflections.

-
-
-
-

In Numbers 27:18-20, God directed Moses to appoint Joshua, a man filled with the Spirit, as his successor, to ensure Israel's continued leadership under God's guidance. God instructed Moses to lay hands on him publicly, which symbolized a transfer of both authority and credibility before the people. The goal was for the people to follow Joshua as they followed Moses.

This divine process shows that leadership transition is not merely organizational, but spiritual and intentional.

Application: Securing the Future & Building Biblically for Impact

As you build biblically and secure the future, it is important to take special note of the following three points:

1. **Leadership Succession Is a Spiritual Responsibility.**
   - It requires preparing Spirit-filled leaders who can continue God's mission beyond the current generation.

2. **Public Affirmation Strengthens Continuity.**
   - It requires affirming new leaders visibly and prayerfully, showing that God's work continues through His chosen servants.

3. **Transfer of Wisdom and Authority Builds Legacy.**
   - It requires seasoned leaders to share their experience, insight, and authority to empower others, which ensures that leadership transitions produce growth, and the mission of God remains strong and effective for generations to come.

6.1 – LEARN: Why Integration Secures the Future

Introduction to LEARN

Imagine holding five strands of rope in your hands. Separately, they are useful, but when carefully woven together, the sum of the parts becomes much stronger because it minimizes breakage, and creates increased capacity to handle heavier loads.

For years, many ministry teams have served in church separately, rather than as a unified team. As a result, the impact they could have made together was diminished. For your team to be effective, offering leadership that is unified matters because it:

- **Eliminates silos.** Your leaders and teams will stop working in disconnected lanes.
- **Multiplies impact.** Each element will reinforce the others, producing compounding results.
- **Creates sustainability.** Your leaders and teams will remain strong through leader transitions and seasons of ministry.
- **Gives clarity.** Your leaders and teams will understand both the "big picture" and their role within it.

Integration is the key difference between short-term activity and long-term impact. You can have vision, discipleship, systems, growth, and outreach, but without integration, they remain disconnected pieces.

A great model to follow is Jesus' discipleship plan. Jesus' legacy was not a program, but a movement of disciples who made disciples.

Biblical Models of Securing the Future

- **Moses & Joshua (Numbers 27:18-20; Deuteronomy 31:7-8)** – Moses laid hands on Joshua and gave him authority before the people, ensuring leadership would continue without disruption.

- **Nehemiah (Nehemiah 7-8)** – Nehemiah rebuilt not just walls, but also the rhythms of worship, leadership, and community that would sustain God's people.

- **Paul & Timothy (2 Timothy 2:2)** – Paul relayed a reproducible model of leadership where he imparted his life to faithful leaders who would equip others.

- **Jesus & the Twelve (Matthew 28:18-20; John 17:4, 18; Acts 1:8)** – Jesus modeled the ultimate succession plan by sharing His own Spirit to empower the disciples to obey His commission.

Why Integration Is Biblical and Practical

Integration reflects God's design for the Church because it shows a unified Body working together for His mission. Scriptures like 1 Corinthians 12:12-27, Romans 12:4-5, and Ephesians 4:16 remind us that while each part of the Body of Christ has a unique role, each individual part is designed to function best in harmony.

Practically, integration prevents fragmentation, aligns people and systems, and sustains leaders. When ministries work together, discipleship flows naturally, resources are maximized, and the church reflects Christ with greater impact. When the church is functioning properly, we will see:

- **Unity in Mission (Philippians 2:2)** – Shared vision leads to shared sacrifice.

- **Efficiency in Ministry (Ephesians 4:16)** – Each part does its work for the whole Body.

- **Continuity in Leadership (Joshua 1:7-9)** – God's mission endures through leadership transitions.

- **Reproducibility in Discipleship (Matthew 28:19-20)** – Jesus' strategy ensures the mission continues until He returns.

Let's reflect again on Jesus' approach from Session Four to refresh our understanding of His discipleship process. Review the chart below entitled *"Jesus' Discipleship Plan"* to see how He intentionally formed and sent leaders.

Jesus' Discipleship Plan ©

Path	Pattern	Passage	Practice
1. Enlist	Jesus invited the disciples to come follow Him.	Matthew 4:18-22; Mark 1:16-20; Luke 5:2-11; John 1:40-43	• Personally invite people to walk alongside you in spiritual growth. • Share your faith story and how following Jesus changed your life. • Create clear next steps for new believers (welcome lunches, discovery classes, etc.).
2. Equip	Jesus invested in a few and taught them God's truth.	Mark 3:14-15; Matthew 5-7; 16:24-27	• Offer regular Bible studies or small groups focused on application. • Provide training for serving, teaching, and sharing the Gospel. • Pair new believers with mature mentors for guidance and accountability.
3. Emulate	Jesus showed them how to live as a Kingdom representative.	John 13:15; Mark 10:44-45; 1 Peter 5:3	• Model integrity, humility, and servanthood in your daily life. • Let others observe your habits of prayer, study, and service. • Be transparent about your struggles and how God shapes you through them.
4. Engage	Jesus allowed them to participate in serving others.	Matthew 15:29-39; Luke 10:1-9; John 6:1-15	• Involve disciples in ministry opportunities early (e.g., outreach, hospitality). • Debrief after service events to reflect on what God taught them. • Encourage hands-on learning through community projects or missions.
5. Encourage	Jesus prayed for their unity and mission, and taught them how to pray while on mission.	John 17:20-23; Matthew 6:9-15; 26:36-46; Luke 11:1-13; 22:40-46	• Pray regularly with and for those you disciple. • Celebrate small wins and spiritual milestones. • Offer words of affirmation and Scripture to strengthen faith during challenges.
6. Empower	Jesus commissioned and sent them out with authority to represent His Kingdom and minister to others, while promising the Spirit's presence and power with them.	Luke 9:1-6; 10:1-9; Matthew 10:1-42; 28:18-20; Acts 1:8	• Give disciples opportunities to lead ministries or mentor others. • Remind them that the Holy Spirit equips and sustains their mission. • Commission them publicly and stay connected for ongoing support.

Just as Jesus modeled in His ministry, when the principles from the previous five sessions are woven together—clarifying leadership, cultivating personal growth, building healthy teams, developing new leaders, and serving the community—the church begins to function with unity, focus, and purpose.

Integration keeps these principles from standing alone. Instead, each one reinforces the others, creating a sustainable leadership culture that fuels discipleship, strengthens leaders, and advances God's Kingdom with lasting impact. When these elements work together:

- Vision fuels discipleship.
- Discipleship shapes systems.
- Systems enable growth.
- Growth fuels outreach.
- Outreach raises and multiplies leaders.

In the same way Jesus prepared His disciples to continue His mission after He ascended, churches must intentionally guide people from simply attending to actively engaging in God's Spirit-led mission both locally and globally.

In Class Group Exercise:

Using the information we learned from Jesus' Model, let's see what happens when there are gaps in your system. Spend some time talking through the Case Study below.

Case Study: Mark The Tenured Leader

Mark has served in his church for 12 years and supervises several volunteers. He is faithful, dependable, and spiritually mature. However, he never received structured onboarding or leadership development—he was simply "plugged into" ministry because he was willing and gifted.

Looking back, Mark realizes:

- He was never formally **ENLISTED**—no one personally invited him, explained expectations, or shared how his role connected to the ministry's mission.
- He was not **EQUIPPED** with consistent training, so he had to figure out most tasks on his own.
- He never had anyone to **EMULATE**, because he did not have a leader modeling healthy rhythms, boundaries, or ministry practices.
- He was rarely **ENGAGED** in meaningful service review, so he never received support to evaluate what was working or not.
- He did receive **ENCOURAGEMENT** from his pastor occasionally.
- He was **EMPOWERED**, but without preparation—he was handed major responsibilities because he was "faithful," not because he was fully developed.

Today, Mark feels tired, has difficulty developing new leaders, and notices his ministry is not producing long-term fruit. He carries the ministry instead of multiplying it.

Points to Ponder:

1. Which 4 E's were missing in Mark's development?

2. What symptoms in his leadership grew directly out of those missing steps?

 **LET'S REFLECT ... LET'S TALK**

Individual Reflection Questions – LEARN

1. Who invested most in shaping my leadership, and what practices did they model?

2. Which "step" of Jesus' blueprint (*Enlist, Equip, Emulate, Engage, Encourage, Empower*) do I practice most naturally? Which step do I often neglect?

3. What is one intentional way I can begin investing in the next generation of leaders this month, and how can I ensure that my tenured leaders are properly developed?

Team Discussion Questions – LEARN

1. Do we have a shared understanding of what constitutes a "ready leader" within our church?

2. Are we identifying potential leaders early enough?

3. How can we make leadership development more relational?

 ## 6.2 – LINK: Connecting the Pieces for Ministry Impact

In this section, you will turn all of your work into a ministry blueprint that your team can use for years to come. The goal is not simply to complete templates, but to understand how each piece fits together to move your mission forward with clarity and unity.

Benefits of Connecting the Pieces

At least four things happen when you and your team connect the pieces:

1. **Clarity** – Ensures everyone understands the direction and how each part contributes to it.
2. **Consistency** – Ensures the same values and goals are consistently reflected in every ministry area.
3. **Momentum** – Ensures there are no ministry hindrances, so that the progress in one area can fuel movement in others.
4. **Reproducibility** – Ensures the plan can be taught, shared, and handed off to future leaders.

Classroom Contextualization Process

Follow the steps below to begin the journey to a healthy and thriving ministry.

 ### Step 1 – Gather All Templates (10 min)

- Vision Clarity Statements, Discipleship Pathway, Systems Audit, Discipleship Growth Plan, Outreach Engagement Plan.

 ### Step 2 – Identify Core Themes (15 min)

- Highlight recurring priorities, values, and strategies across your plans.

 Step 3 – Check for Alignment (15 min)

- Ensure that each plan supports your vision and mission without contradiction.

 Step 4 – Create Your Integration Summary (10 min)

- Write a one-page summary, double-spaced, explaining your overall leadership strategy, linking all RPG elements.

 # LET'S REFLECT ... LET'S TALK

Individual Reflection Questions – LINK

1. Which part of my leadership plan feels strongest?

2. Which part needs more work before presenting it?

3. How do these pieces serve the overall mission God has given me?

Team Discussion Questions – LINK

1. Do all our ministry systems and strategies point in the same direction?

2. How do we communicate this integration to volunteers and leaders?

3. What changes will we make immediately after today?

 ## 6.3 – LEAD: Presenting Your Leadership Plan

Introduction to LEAD

This final step gives you the opportunity to bring all your learning together into a clear, integrated leadership strategy. It serves as both a clarity check, and as a chance to gain feedback before full implementation. The goal is not perfection, but growth. This time will help you refine your vision, clarifying your next steps and strengthening your plan through shared insight.

Follow the steps below to prepare your presentation. Afterwards, we will discuss this exercise together.

Action Steps & Workshop Activity – Leadership Presentation (40 min)

 ### Step 1 – Prepare Your Presentation (10 min)

- Take time to gather your notes and organize your plan. Included in your plan should be your:

  > **Vision:** What will success look like in 6-12 months if your plan is implemented?

  > **Mission:** What is the spiritual or practical purpose driving your ministry?

  > **Key Strategies:** What are your top 2-3 priorities or actions that affect your top principles?

  > **Next Step:** What will you do in the next 30-60 days to put this plan into action?

Tip: For this section, use some sort of visual aids to help students see your structure.

 ### Step 2 – Deliver to Your Group (20 min)

- Each participant has 5-7 minutes to present their leadership plan with their table or small group.

 Step 3 – Peer Feedback (10 min)

- List two strengths and one improvement suggestion for each presentation.

 # LET'S REFLECT ... LET'S TALK

Individual Reflection Questions – LEAD

1. How clearly did I communicate my strategy?

2. What feedback was most valuable?

3. What will I adjust before launching this plan in my ministry?

Team Discussion Questions – LINK

1. Which ideas from other presentations could strengthen our ministry?

2. How can we support one another in implementation?

3. How will we hold each other accountable to act on our plans?

Suggested Tools & Resources

- All Templates from previous months

- Church Unique by Will Mancini

- Presentation outline samples (RPG Resource)

NOTE: Scan the QR code on page 111 to download the RPG templates.

 ## 6.4 – L.E.A.D.S.S. In Action

1. Deliver your leadership plan to your ministry team.
2. Begin implementing one major action step from the plan.
3. Schedule a follow-up meeting with your RPG coach.

End Notes

Session 6 - Endnotes (Secure The Future)

1. Myles Munroe, *The Principle of Legacy: Leaving Something Behind*

2. John C. Maxwell, *Developing the Leader Within You 2.0* (Nashville, TN: HarperCollins Leadership, 2018).

3. Key Scripture references cited throughout Session 6 include: Numbers 27:18-20; Deuteronomy 31:7-8; Nehemiah 7 - 8; 2 Timothy 2:2; Matthew 28:18-20; John 17:4, 18; Acts 1:8; 1 Corinthians 12:12-27; Romans 12:4-5; Ephesians 4:16; Philippians 2:2; Joshua 1:7-9.

4. Concepts of succession, leadership development, pipelines, and identification, missional leadership, ministry sustainability, and integrated systems in this session were generally influenced by:

   - Alan Hirsch, *The Forgotten Ways* (Grand Rapids, MI: Brazos Press, 2016).
   - Aubrey Malphurs, *Being Leaders* (Grand Rapids, MI: Baker Books, 2003).
   - Aubrey Malphurs, *Developing Leaders for the 21st Century* (Grand Rapids, MI: Baker Books, 2004).
   - Eric Geiger & Kevin Peck, *Designed to Lead* (Nashville, TN: B&H Publishing, 2016).
   - John C. Maxwell, *The 21 Irrefutable Laws of Leadership* (Nashville, TN: Thomas Nelson, 2007).
   - Myles Munroe, *The Spirit of Leadership* (New Kensington, PA: Whitaker House, 2005).

My Notes

Closing Remarks

Congratulations on completing the L.E.A.D.S.S. leadership journey. Over the past six sessions, you have prayed, studied, planned, evaluated, and built, brick by brick, a sustainable, disciple-shaping, Kingdom-advancing leadership framework. You have clarified vision, equipped disciples, aligned systems, designed pathways for growth, embraced mission beyond the walls, and created plans to secure the future. This was not just training, it was transformation. You did not simply learn principles, you built a foundation for generational impact.

As you move forward, remember that leadership development is not a finished assignment, but a lifelong calling. The true measure of your leadership will not be seen only in what you build, but in those you build up, leaders who will continue the mission when your season is complete. You are leaving footprints for those who will follow, and seeds for those who will lead after you.

About The Authors

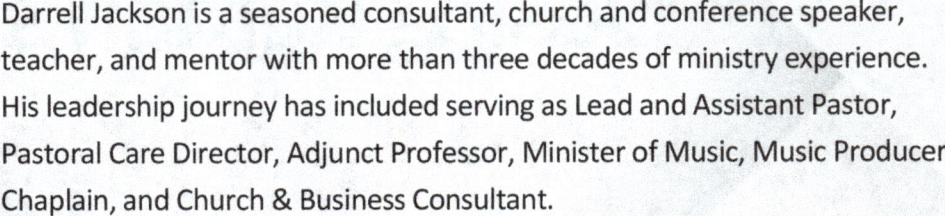

Darrell Jackson

Darrell Jackson is a seasoned consultant, church and conference speaker, teacher, and mentor with more than three decades of ministry experience. His leadership journey has included serving as Lead and Assistant Pastor, Pastoral Care Director, Adjunct Professor, Minister of Music, Music Producer, Chaplain, and Church & Business Consultant.

As the founder of Raise Performance Group and The Equippers Theological Institute, Darrell designs and delivers biblical training that helps pastors and leaders thrive in their calling.

He holds a Bachelor's degree in Christian Leadership and a Master of Divinity. He is also a certified DISC trainer with additional leadership credentials. As author of the L.E.A.D.S.S. curriculum, Darrell brings together his passion for systems, leadership development, and theology to equip leaders to lead with clarity, disciple intentionally, align systems for health, and secure a Spirit-led future for the church.

Bryant Lee, Sr.

Bryant Lee, Sr., is the founding and Lead Pastor of Higher Expectations Church in Humble, Texas, and also serves as a Church Consultant with over two decades of ministry experience. He mentors bi-vocational pastors and urban leaders, offering pastoral wisdom and missional focus to equip and empower emerging leaders.

A U.S. Army veteran, Bryant's life and ministry reflect a deep commitment to discipline, resilience, and servant leadership. He holds degrees in Bible Studies and Multidisciplinary Studies, as well as a Master of Theology.

As co-author of the L.E.A.D.S.S. curriculum, Bryant integrates pastoral experience, military precision, and mentoring insight to help leaders grow in both character and competence, while advancing God's mission through effective and faithful leadership.

Shared Passion for Equipping Leaders

Darrell Jackson and Bryant Lee, Sr., combine decades of leadership experience with a shared passion to help leaders lead well, live well, love well, and leave a lasting Kingdom legacy.

Contact Us

Thank you for engaging in the L.E.A.D.S.S. leadership journey. If you have questions, would like coaching support, or want to bring this training to your ministry or organization, contact us at:

Raise Performance Group

PO BOX 709, Fresno, Texas 77545

Email: info@raiseperformancegroup.com

Website: www.raiseperformancegroup.com

We look forward to partnering with you as you raise leaders who will make a lasting Kingdom impact for generations to come.

Scan this QR Code to receive additional leadership resources, and to gain access to the RPG Templates that you will use in each session.

07 Reference List & Works Cited

The concepts in each chapter were shaped by insights from several biblical leadership and discipleship authors whose writings have informed our understanding of spiritual formation and leadership development. They include:

Biblical References

- The Holy Bible, English Standard Version (ESV). Wheaton, IL: Crossway, 2016.
- The Holy Bible, New International Version (NIV). Grand Rapids, MI: Zondervan, 2011.
- The Holy Bible, New King James Version (NKJV). Thomas Nelson, 1982.
- The Holy Bible, New American Standard Version (NASB 1995). Grand Rapids: Lockman 1995.

Primary Books and Leadership Resources Consulted

- Addington, T.J. Leading from the Sandbox. Colorado Springs, CO: NavPress, 2010.
- Bailey, E.K. Living and Preaching Biblical Truth. EK Bailey Ministries, various sermons & writings.
- Blanchard, Ken, and Renee Broadwell, eds. Servant Leadership in Action. Oakland, CA: Berrett-Koehler Publishers, 2018.
- Browning, Dave , Deliberate Simplicity: Creating Simplicity in Your Church. Grand Rapids, MI: Zondervan, 2009.
- Evans, Tony. The Kingdom Agenda: Life Under God. Moody Publishers, 2010.
- Evans, Tony. Kingdom Disciples: Heaven's Representatives on Earth. Moody Publishers, 2018.
- Francis, Chan, and Mark Beuving, Multiply: Disciples Making Disciples. Colorado Springs: David C Cook, 2012.
- Harari, Oren. The Leadership Secrets of Colin Powell. New York, NY: McGraw-Hill, 2002.
- Hindley, John. Serving Without Sinking: How to Serve Christ and Keep Your Joy. Epsom, UK: The Good Book Company, 2013.
- Loritts, Crawford W. Jr. Leadership as an Identity: The Four Traits of Those Who Wield Lasting Influence. Chicago, IL: Moody Publishers, 2009.
- Mancini, Will. Church Unique: How Missional Leaders Cast Vision, Capture Culture, and Create Movement. Jossey-Bass, 2008.

Reference List & Works Cited

Primary Books and Leadership Resources Consulted Continued

- Maxwell, John C. The 21 Irrefutable Laws of Leadership: Follow Them and People Will Follow You. Nashville, TN: Thomas Nelson, 2007.
- Munroe, Myles. The Power of Vision. Whitaker House, 2003.
- Ogden, Greg. Transforming Discipleship: Making Disciples a Few at a Time. InterVarsity Press, 2003.
- Patterson, A. Louis. Sermons & teachings.
- Putman, Jim, Bobby Harrington, and Robert E. Coleman. Discipleshift: Five Steps That Help Your Church Make Disciples Who Make Disciples. Grand Rapids, MI: Zondervan, 2013.
- Rainer, Thom S., and Eric Geiger. Simple Church: Returning to God's Process for Making Disciples. Nashville, TN: B&H Publishing Group, 2006.
- Sanders, J. Oswald. Spiritual Leadership. Moody Publishers, 2007.
- Scazzero, Peter. The Emotionally Healthy Leader. Grand Rapids, MI: Zondervan, 2015.
- Thurman, Howard. Jesus and the Disinherited. Beacon Press, 1996.
- Trotman, Dawson. Born to Reproduce. Colorado Springs, CO: NavPress, 1955.

Additional Books and Leadership Resources Consulted

- Blackaby, Henry, and Richard Blackaby. Spiritual Leadership: Moving People on to God's Agenda. B&H Publishing, 2011.
- Blanchard, Ken, and Mark Miller. The Secret. San Francisco, CA: Berrett-Koehler Publishers, 2004.
- Bowser, Kevin E. The Emotionally Agile Leader. Dallas, TX: Bowser Publishing, 2017.
- Breen, Mike. Building a Discipling Culture. 3DM Publishing, 2017.
- Chand, Sam, and Gerald Brooks. Ladder Focus. Dallas, TX: SCLI, 2019.
- Coleman, Robert E. The Master Plan of Evangelism. Revell, 2010.
- Cone, James H. A Black Theology of Liberation. Orbis Books, 1986.
- Damazio, Frank. Effective Keys to Successful Leadership. Portland, OR: City Christian Publishing, 1988.
- Damazio, Frank. Life-Changing Leadership. Portland, OR: City Christian Publishing, 2005.

Additional Books and Leadership Resources Consulted Continued

- Damazio, Frank. Strategic Church. Ventura, CA: Regal Books, 2012.
- Ellis, Carl F. Jr. Free at Last? The Gospel in the African-American Experience. InterVarsity Press, 1996.
- Evans, Tony. Kingdom Focused Church. Moody Publishers, 2003.
- Evans, Tony. The Kingdom Agenda: Life Under God. Moody Publishers, 2006.
- Hartwig, Ryan T., and Warren Bird. Teams That Thrive. Downers Grove, IL: InterVarsity Press, 2015.
- Hilliard, Donald Jr. Church Growth from an African American Perspective. Valley Forge, PA: Judson Press, 1994.
- Hirsch, Alan. The Forgotten Ways. Brazos Press, 2016.
- Hyatt, Michael, and Daniel Harkavy. Living Forward. Grand Rapids, MI: Baker Books, 2016.
- Geiger, Eric and Kevin Peck, Designed to Lead (Nashville, TN: B&H Publishing, 2016).
- Gray, Derwin L. The High Definition Leader: Building Multiethnic Churches in a Multiethnic World. Thomas Nelson, 2015.
- Keller, Timothy. Center Church: Doing Balanced, Gospel-Centered Ministry in Your City. Zondervan, 2012.
- Kreider, Larry. Passing the 21 Tests of Leadership: Biblical Insights for Leaving a Legacy of Leadership and Influence. Lititz, PA: DOVE International, 2018.
- Lencioni, Patrick. The Advantage: Why Organizational Health Trumps Everything Else in Business. Jossey-Bass, 2012.
- Malphurs, Aubrey. Being Leaders (Grand Rapids, MI: Baker Books, 2003).
- Malphurs, Aubrey. Developing Leaders for the 21st Century (Grand Rapids, MI: Baker Books, 2004).
- Marshall, Colin, and Tony Payne. The Vine Project. Kingsford, Australia: Matthias Media, 2016.
- Mason, Eric. Woke Church: An Urgent Call for Christians in America to Confront Racism and Injustice. Moody Publishers, 2018.
- Maxwell, John C. Developing the Leader Within You 2.0. HarperCollins Leadership, 2018.
- Miller, Mark. The Secret of Teams. San Francisco, CA: Berrett-Koehler Publishers, 2011.
- Perkins, John M. Let Justice Roll Down. Baker Books, 2010.
- Perkins, John M. One Blood: Parting Words to the Church on Race and Love. Moody Publishers, 2018.

07

Reference List & Works Cited

Additional Books and Leadership Resources Consulted Continued

- Scazzero, Peter. Emotionally Healthy Spirituality. Grand Rapids, MI: Zondervan, 2017.
- Searcy, Nelson. The Renegade Pastor. Grand Rapids, MI: Baker Books, 2013.
- Stanley, Andy. Deep & Wide: Creating Churches Unchurched People Love to Attend. Zondervan, 2012.
- Stanley, Andy, and Lane Jones. Communicating for a Change. Multnomah, 2006.
- Thomas, Luke. Leadership Durability. Houston, TX: Self-Published, 2021.
- Thurman, Howard. Disciplines of the Spirit. Friends United Press, 1963.
- Whitney, Donald S. Spiritual Disciplines for the Christian Life. NavPress, 2014.
- Willard, Dallas. The Divine Conspiracy: Rediscovering Our Hidden Life in God. HarperCollins, 1998.

Additional Ministry & Systems Resources Consulted

- Barna, George. Growing True Disciples. WaterBrook Press, 2001.
- Heifetz, Ronald A. Leadership Without Easy Answers. Harvard University Press, 1994.
- Mancini, Will. God Dreams: 12 Vision Templates for Finding and Focusing Your Church's Future. B&H Publishing, 2016.
- Stetzer, Ed, and David Putman. Breaking the Missional Code. B&H Publishing, 2006.
- Welch, Robert H. Church Administration. Nashville, TN: B&H Academic, 2011.

General Works Referenced

- Bonhoeffer, Dietrich. Life Together. HarperOne, 2009.
- Goleman, Daniel. "What Makes a Leader?" Harvard Business Review 76, no. 6 (1998): 93-102.
- Robinson, Haddon W. Biblical Preaching. Baker Academic, 2001.